INTELLGENCE'S CREATIVE MULTIPLICITY

Also by Charles Johnston:

The Creative Imperative: Human Growth and Planetary Evolution

Necessary Wisdom: Meeting the Challenge of a New Cultural Maturity

Pattern and Reality: A Brief Introduction to Creative Systems Theory

The Power of Diversity: An Introduction to the Creative Systems Personality Typology

An Evolutionary History of Music: Introducing Creative Systems Theory Through the Language of Sound (DVD)

Quick and Dirty Answers to the Biggest of Questions: Creative Systems Theory Explains What It Is All About (Really)

Cultural Maturity: A Guidebook for the Future

Hope and the Future: Confronting Today's Crisis of Purpose

On the Evolution of Intimacy: A Brief Exploration into the Past, Present, and Future of Gender and Love

Rethinking How We Think: Integrative Meta-Perspective and the Cognitive "Growing Up" on Which Our Future Depends

Creative Systems Theory: A Comprehensive Theory of Purpose, Change, and Interrelationship in Human Systems (with Particular Pertinence to Understanding the Times We Live in and the Tasks Ahead for the Species)

Perspective and Guidance for a Time of Deep Discord: Why We See Such Extreme Social and Political Polarization—and What We Can Do About It

Insight: Creative Systems Theory's Radical New Picture of Human Possibility

Online:

Author/professional page: www.CharlesJohnstonMD.com

The Institute for Creative Development: www.CreativeSystems.org

Creative Systems Theory: www.CSTHome.org

An Evolutionary History of Music: www.Evolmusic.org

Cultural Maturity Blog: www.CulturalMaturityBlog.net

Looking to the Future podcast: LookingToTheFuture.net

Ask the Cultural Psychiatrist YouTube channel: youtube.com/@cjohnstonmd

CHARLES M. JOHNSTON, MD

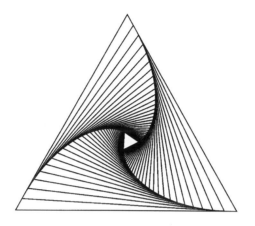

INTELLGENCE'S
CREATIVE
MULTIPLICITY

AND ITS CRITICAL ROLE IN THE
FUTURE OF UNDERSTANDING

The Institute for Creative Development (ICD) Press
Seattle, Washington

Publisher's Cataloging-In-Publication Data

Names: Johnston, Charles M., author.

Title: Intelligence's creative multiplicity : and it's critical role in the future of understanding / Charles M. Johnston, MD.

Description: Seattle, Washington : The Institute for Creative Development (ICD) Press, [2023] |

Includes bibliographical references and index.

Identifiers: ISBN: 978-1-7342431-6-1 (print) | 978-1-7342431-7-8 (ebook) |

LCCN: 2021924744

Subjects: LCSH: Intellect. | Cognition. | Comprehension. | Consciousness. | Civilization, Modern--Psychological aspects. | Conduct of life. | Social evolution.

Classification: LCC: BF431 .J64 2023 | DDC: 153.9--dc23

The Institute for Creative Development (ICD) Press, Seattle, Washington

Cover design by Safeer Ahmed

Author photo by Brad Kevelin

ISBN: 978-1-7342431-6-1

Library of Congress Control Number: 2021924744

First printing 2023

INTELLGENCE'S CREATIVE MULTIPLICITY

How Much We Miss

Human intelligence is truly amazing. But in our time, we commonly fail to recognize its full richness. When we use the word "intelligence," our immediate association is to logic and rationality. While we appropriately celebrate our rationality, in fact it represents only one part of intelligence's deep workings. By itself, it fails to explain what makes us endlessly creative, crafters not just of tools, but also of great works of art and the structures of civilizations. It also fails to explain what makes possible a complexity of social interaction not found with other species. In fact, as we shall see, by itself it fails to explain the larger portion of what gives human life vitality and meaning.

Historical perspective helps us appreciate why today we view intelligence as we do. It also begins to bring intelligence's larger picture into focus. It turns out that at previous times in the human story, not only have other aspects of our cognitive complexity been just as recognized, often they have served as intelligence's primary voice. For example, in tribal societies, the intelligence of the body stands forefront. Understanding at its most basic is communicated through drumbeat, song, and dance. With the early rise of civilizations, the language of myth and symbol came to have new prominence. Understanding then was voiced by pantheons of gods and through great mythic tales. And, later still, understanding's primary manifestations became more emotional and moral. We find this with the ascent of the great monotheistic religions in both the West and the East.

Equating intelligence with rationality is in fact quite new. We appropriately associate it with René Descartes' "I think, therefore I am." We recognize intimations with earlier times. The philosophies of Plato and Aristotle certainly drew strongly on the rational. But what we encountered then was different in important ways from what we today associate with "using one's head." Aristotle, as with most people of his time, assumed that the mind was located in the heart.

In our time, we tend to equate logic and rationality not just with intelligence, but with truth. That we do is understandable. With each previous major period in culture's story, we've assumed that its ordering intelligence defined truth. And certainly rationality's rise was a profound achievement. A new supremacy for rational intelligence was key to the leap in understanding that gave us Modern Age thought and all that has followed from it—the scientific revolution, modern higher education, liberal monotheism, representative democracy, and all the institutions we rely on in contemporary society. With the Renaissance and the later Age of Reason, we were able to put the mysticism and irrationality of times past behind us and proclaim our place as rational and objective beings.

Today, we tend to think of where this progression has taken us as an ideal and end point. Here I will propose that it is not an end point, or at least that it can't be an end point if we are to continue to advance as a species. I will describe how the tasks before us as a species are demanding that we draw in a newly conscious way on the whole of cognition's workings. Moving forward effectively will require that we engage intelligence's multiplicity with an encompassing completeness that has not before been an option.

We reside at an awkward in-between place with this kind of recognition. More often than not today, even the best of thinkers fail to fully appreciate the deep workings of intelligence, in particular its multifaceted nature. But it is also the case that we've made significant steps over the last century toward acknowledging the need for a larger picture. We hear educators debating whether IQ adequately measures the whole of intelligence. Medicine is beginning to recognize how mind and body, far from being separate worlds, interlink through a complex array of communications molecules. And we find intelligence's traditional picture challenged even in the hardest of the hard sciences. I think of physicist Niels Bohr's famous assertion that, "when it comes to atoms, language can be used only as in poetry."

We've also seen important efforts toward delineating today's needed more differentiated (and integrated) picture of intelligence. The neurosciences have replaced old images of a single managerial, rational brain with a view that recognizes multiple quasi-independent "brains"—in one familiar interpretation, a reptilian brain and a mammalian brain, capped with that thin outer cerebral layer in which we humans take special and appropriate pride. Educational theorists offer an array of interpretations, the most well known being Howard Gardner's seven-part smorgasbord of intelligences.[1] The popular assertion that we need to think with "both sides of the brain," while neurologically simplistic, draws our attention to how the task is not just to have lots of intelligences at our disposal, but to find ways in which various aspects of how we make sense of things might more consciously work together.

Here I will draw specifically on the approach put forward by Creative Systems Theory (CST), the body of conceptual work that underlies much of my life's contribution.[2] The theory provides overarching perspective for understanding

---

1 We will take a closer look in Chapter Two.

2 Charles M. Johnston, MD, *Creative Systems Theory: A Comprehensive Theory of Purpose, Change, and Interrelationship in Human Systems (with Particular Pertinence to Understanding the Times We Live In and the Tasks Ahead for the Species)*, ICD Press, 2021.

how we understand, and how we do so differently at different times and places. The concept of Cultural Maturity, a key notion within the theory, addresses how the times in which we live are requiring that we bring a systemic sophistication to how we understand that has not before been necessary or possible. Cultural Maturity involves changes not just in what we think, but in how we think—specific cognitive changes. These changes offer that we might at once more fully step back from and more deeply engage the whole of our cognitive complexity. The fact that intelligence is multiple provides one of the best ways to think about that complexity.

Creative Systems Theory's framing of intelligence's multiplicity represents only one strategy, but it proves particularly powerful. The theory proposes that our toolmaking nature means that human intelligence must, at the least, effectively support innovation. And it goes on to describe how our various intelligences—or we might better say "sensibilities," to reflect all they encompass—relate in specifically creative ways. The detailed framework that results expands understanding in ways critical to our time. By delineating how particular ways of knowing, and particular relationships between ways of knowing, predominate at specific times in any human developmental process, the theory helps us better understand change and offers that we might be more intelligent in the face of change. By tying the underlying structures of intelligence to patterns we see in how human systems relate, it invites us to relate in more mature and creative ways. And of particular importance, the specifically generative picture of intelligence's complexity the theory provides helps us grasp just what our times are asking of us as intelligent beings.

My purpose with this book is to offer the reader an encompassing and practical picture of intelligence and its richness. In doing so, I will attempt to clarify why realizing the more complete—we could say simply, wise—kind of thinking and acting that our future requires depends on better drawing on intelligence's multiplicity. I will also describe how the capacity to better hold the whole of intelligence is not just some ideal to be hoped for. At least its potential is built into our natures as creative—toolmaking, meaning-making—beings.

CHAPTER ONE

Multiple Intelligences and Our Time's Creative Imperative

Attempting to make sense of intelligence's multiple aspects played a key early role in my thinking. In my youth, I found special interest in artistic creation, particularly sculpting and the making of music. Eventually I found increasing fascination with creative process itself, with just how new things come into being.

At that time, intelligence's multiplicity was only beginning to be acknowledged. With my inquiries into creative process, I was struck by how creative dynamics of all sorts drew on a variety of different ways of knowing and did so in specific ways at different points along the way. I observed how the intelligence of the body had particular importance with the "inklings" that alert us to creativity's germinal beginnings, how the intelligence of imagination and symbol moves forefront as a newly created object emerges into the light, how emotional intelligence plays the larger role with the hard work of making new creation manifest, and how rationality takes new importance with the task of bringing the work to completion.

Those inquiries also made clear that I would need to give some special attention to intelligence's more creatively germinal sensibilities—its kinesthetic/bodily aspects and also its more imagination/symbol-making aspects. At our time in culture, these dimensions of intelligence tend to be particularly foreign to us. If people are conscious of such sensibilities at all, they tend not to think of them as intelligence. Work I then did with Joseph Campbell, one of our time's most respected chroniclers of myth and symbol,[1] and Stanley Keleman, an early innovator in body-related psychotherapeutic approaches,[2] helped me fill out my understanding of the role of intelligence's more germinal aspects in creativity's workings.

Over time, I came to recognize how the fact that intelligence had multiple aspects had broader implications. As I was introduced in my training to developmental psychology—and in particular, more systemic developmental thinkers such as Jean Piaget[3] and Lawrence Kohlberg[4]—I was struck by how an acknowledgement of intelligence's multiple aspects was needed to at all deeply understand individual development. I also saw that essential parallels existed between how intelligence's multiplicity worked over the course of individual development and what I had observed for creative dynamics. And of particular significance, with time I came to recognize the related importance of intelligence's multiplicity with the evolution of culture that I made reference to in the Preface. Reflecting on parallels between how intelligence's multiple aspects play out over the course of generative processes at all of these levels—from a simple creative act, to individual human growth, to the evolution of human understanding—provided the starting point for the development of Creative Systems Theory.

Key with cultural-level observations—and of particular pertinence to the topic of intelligence's multiplicity—was coming to appreciate the cultural change-point that Creative Systems Theory calls Cultural Maturity. The theory proposes that our times are demanding—and making possible—a new chapter in our human development, an essential kind of

---

1 Joseph Campbell, *The Power of Myth*, Anchor Books, 1991.

2 Stanley Keleman, *Your Body Speaks Its Mind*, Center Press, 1975.

3 Jean Piaget, *The Language and Thought of the Child*, London: Routledge & Kegan Paul, 1926.

4 Lawrence Kohlberg, *The Meaning and Measurement of Moral Development*, Harper and Row, 1984.

"growing up" as a species. And it ties these changes to more
mature stages in culture as a creative process. Throughout
history, we've related to culture as a mythic parent. We've
also relied on ideological beliefs rooted in particular aspects
of our cognitive complexity. The concept of Cultural Maturity describes how our times are making it possible to bring a
new, more encompassing kind of understanding to concerns
of all sorts, one that gets beyond both parental mythic pro-
jections and more limited ideological assumptions and better
engages experience from the entirety of ourselves.

The cognitive changes that produce this essential new
step in how we understand both highlight the importance
of intelligence's creative multiplicity and clarify how a more
encompassing relationship to it might be possible. Culturally
mature systemic perspective applies our intelligence in the
rational sense with particular precision. But it also in some
way necessarily draws on every other aspect of intelligence.
Culturally mature thought links facts with feelings, the workings of the imagination with more practical considerations,
and observations of the mind with things only our bodies can
know.

The dynamics of maturity in our individual lives support
this pivotal role for intelligence's multiplicity in needed
cultural-level changes. We associate the best of thinking in
our later years not just with knowledge, but with wisdom.
Knowledge can be articulated quite well by the intellect
alone. But wisdom requires that we draw on the whole of
who we are. We see it not just because we better include all
the aspects of our questions, but also because, when seeking
answers, we don't leave out essential parts of ourselves. If the
concept of Cultural Maturity is correct, we should expect an
analogous result at a species level. And it is essential that
we do. The future will require something beyond just being
smarter in the decisions we make. Given the magnitude of
the choices we confront and the potential consequences if
we choose poorly, it is critical that our decisions be not just
intelligent, but wise.

Two Ways We Can Miss the Mark

Ideas about intelligence can miss the mark in a couple of opposite ways that are important to appreciate in getting started. Each at different times has worked to stop me in my tracks in my efforts to better understand and communicate a more creative and complete picture of intelligence.

The first is most common. Particularly in academic settings, people can fail to recognize that anything beyond the rational exists, or at least exists as intelligence. I confronted this obstacle in my early efforts to explore creative process. When in medical school, I brought together a group of some of the most innovative professors at the University of Washington to serve as a committee for a parallel, independent PhD on the topic of creativity. After a few meetings, several members gave me some advice that I did not at first welcome. They suggested that academia would likely not be the most fruitful place to pursue my interest. They observed that academic thought, at least to that point, didn't have a great deal to say about creative process. They also noted that because academia hadn't given the topic serious consideration, even if I made solid progress in my efforts, my contributions would likely not be appreciated. This might be different in certain settings today, but not greatly different.

The reason for this circumstance helps put academia's relationship to the larger topic of intelligence's multiplicity in perspective. While we might easily expect academia to be the place to go to learn about intelligence's multiple aspects, most often it will fail us in this regard. Higher education as we know it came into being with Modern Age thought. Since then, it has existed to prepare people to thrive and prosper in a world in which Modern Age values and ways of thinking prevailed. With formal education, understanding is rational understanding. Higher education is interested in "objective" truth. This is not to say that there aren't classes that touch on more subjective concerns—most all universities have departments for the arts and humanities. But such pursuits tend to have secondary status. The arts in our time are seen more as decoration than anything related to substantive inquiry. And as often as not the arts and humanities are reduced to "criticism" in a way that makes them again but rational enterprises.

I will touch on several unfortunate results that follow from this reality in later chapters. Most immediately, higher education fails to effectively address concerns that don't easily fit into this limited worldview, many of which—such as meaning, love, or spirituality (along with creativity)—have particular significance in our lives. We will also see how this circumstance leaves higher education without the ability to address many topics that it considers its purview—such as history or human identity—with needed depth. We will see too how it makes higher education a poor place to learn for people whose temperaments do not draw predominantly on rational intelligence—indeed, often an inhospitable place. And I will give particular emphasis to a conclusion that might seem ironic given how we tend to think of higher education's role in society. It means that higher education makes a much smaller contribution to the kind of thinking needed for the future than we might hope.

But identifying with rationality is not the only way that our thinking can fall short when it comes to intelligence's creative multiplicity. People can also miss the mark from an opposite direction. They can identify with the nonrational and polarize against the rational. Appreciating this second kind of trap is just as important for this book's inquiry. It has confronted me in my work as often as the first and has had a major effect on how I have come to approach the topic of intelligence's multiplicity.

For twenty years I directed the Institute for Creative Development, a Seattle-based think tank and center for advanced leadership training. I would often begin trainings with exercises that immersed people experientially into the various modes of intelligence as understood by Creative Systems Theory. (We will explore intelligence's multiplicity in this way in Chapter Three.) For most people, this proved to be a particularly accessible and effective way to engage the needed larger cognitive picture. But for certain people this was not the result. If a person's makeup or belief systems tended toward a dismissing of the rational, my efforts would only end up reinforcing such dismissal. It is a kind of trap that gets new converts with the current rise of liberal populism, with New Age spiritual beliefs, and with the more simplistic of postmodern sentiments. The poets rather than the intellectuals become the ones who really know. While a person might think that explanation would provide a simple way to address this second kind of trap, the fact that such thinking identifies with rationality's opposite makes it particularly impervious to questioning.

This second kind of trap has had a major impact on how I go about introducing intelligence-related ideas. Because certain people can so readily—and often intractably—confuse an emphasis on intelligence's multiplicity with some opposite to rationality, I have reluctantly stopped making this kind of hands-on approach a starting point with my teaching. For the same reason, I have not written in real depth about multiple intelligences since my first book, *The Creative Imperative*.[5] Nonrational aspects of intelligence are hard enough to write about for the simple reason that they don't as well conform to written language. But it is also the case that the effort can be easily misinterpreted and undermined.

Both of these kinds of traps necessarily confront us if we wish to engage intelligence in its entirety. And, today, as people more and more often take sides with polarities of every sort, each kind of trap in its own way becomes an even greater obstacle to the needed more complete kind of understanding.[6] But bringing intelligence's larger picture

---

5 Charles M. Johnston, MD, *The Creative Imperative: Human Growth and Planetary Evolution*, Celestial Arts, 1984.

6 Each kind of trap reflects a more general way that our thinking can go astray. Creative Systems Theory describes how a defining

alive has become so inescapably important that engaging the challenge has become well worth another try. Learning to draw on the whole of intelligence in our time has come to have a kind of significance that cannot be ignored.

Integrative Meta-Perspective

Before diving in and more directly exploring the various aspects of intelligence's creative multiplicity, we benefit from a few further big-picture reflections. Some of them will be more conceptual than many readers will find immediately useful. And they are not needed for the book's basic observations to provide value. But many people will find them of particular value. It is important that we have a solid grasp of why engaging intelligence with the needed greater completeness is becoming essential. It is important, too, that we recognize how it is that the ability to do so is becoming an option.

A closer look at the cognitive reordering that produces Cultural Maturity helps more solidly establish the significance of its changes in culture's story and to tie them more specifically to intelligence. The term that Creative Systems Theory uses to describe the results of these changes—Integrative Meta-

---

characteristic of culturally mature understanding is that it "bridges"—draws a systemic circle around—past defining polar relationships (such as mind and body, masculine and feminine, political right and political left, or in this case, rational and nonrational). It identifies three kinds of polar fallacies, ways of thinking that fail at this task. It calls them Separation Fallacies, Unity Fallacies, and Compromise Fallacies. Separation Fallacies identify with difference. Unity Fallacies identify with oneness. And Compromise Fallacies confuse systemic completeness with splitting the differences. We can use this framing to understand traps that we confront when engaging the topic of intelligence's multiplicity. The common equating of intelligence with rationality represents a Separation Fallacy. Identifying with rationality's opposite replaces Separation Fallacies with Unity Fallacies (or sometimes Compromise Fallacies).

perspective[7]—is a mouthful. But it gets at what is involved with regard to intelligence quite precisely. I've observed how Cultural Maturity's cognitive changes involve at once more fully stepping back from and more deeply engaging our human complexity. I've also observed how thinking of that complexity in terms of intelligence's creative multiplicity provides one of the best ways to understand what is involved.

Modern Age thought similarly had its origins in a new kind of cognitive orientation. And stepping back from previous ways of knowing was a big part of it. We became better able to step back from the more mystical sensibilities that gave us the beliefs of the Middle Ages. Along with this more general stepping back, rationality came to have a newly central significance. The rational now stood clearly separate from the subjective aspects of experience and became specifically allied with conscious awareness. The result was a new, as-if-from-a-balcony sense of clarity and objectivity. This, combined with the new belief in the individual as logical choice-maker that accompanied it, produced all the great advances of the Modern Age.

But while Modern Age thought was a grand achievement, the kind of stepping back that comes with Integrative Meta-perspective represents a wholly different sort of accomplishment. Awareness comes to stand more fully separate from the whole of intelligence's systemic complexity—including the rational. Integrative Meta-perspective offers that we might step back equally from aspects of ourselves that before we might have treated as objective and those that we have before thought of as subjective. In the process, it offers that we might better step back from the whole of intelligence. And there is more. Culturally mature understanding involves not just being aware that intelligence has multiple aspects, but that in a whole new sense

7   Charles M. Johnston, MD, *Rethinking How We Think: Integrative Meta-Perspective and the Cognitive "Growing Up" on Which Our Future Depends*, ICD Press, 2020.

we embody each of these aspects. It directly draws on all of our diverse ways of knowing.

Integrative Meta-perspective involves thinking in a rational sense—indeed, it expands rationality's role—but just as much it requires that we more directly plumb the more feeling, imagining, and sensing aspects of who we are. And this is the case as much for the most rigorous of hard theory as when our concerns are more personal. Think of a box of crayons with its many hues. Integrative Meta-perspective challenges us to consciously engage and draw on the whole box. Making deep sense of most anything about us—the values we hold, the mechanisms of human relationship, the nature of individual identity, or the structures that order how we think—ultimately requires this more encompassing and complete kind of understanding.

Why It Is Important

Creative Systems Theory highlights a handful of ways that Integrative Meta-perspective and its new and deeper engagement with intelligence's creative multiplicity have become critical. Each will have an important place in these reflections.

Most immediately, by making a concept like Cultural Maturity possible, Integrative Meta-perspective provides a new kind of guiding narrative. In my writing, I give considerable attention to what I call our modern Crisis of Purpose. With growing frequency, people today find themselves wandering aimlessly without a solid sense of direction in their lives. Postmodern thought's challenging of cultural absolutes has provided a first step beyond Modern Age assumptions. But too easily postmodern thinking leads to anything-goes, everybody-gets-their-own-truth conclusions that fail to offer anything of substance to replace what it insightfully takes away. In the next chapter, I will come back to how Cultural Maturity's cognitive reordering and the more systemic relationship to understanding that results works as an antidote to our time's Crisis of Purpose.

Just how it might relates directly to how Integrative Meta-perspective helps us tap the full depth and complexity of intelligence's workings.

There is also how Integrative Meta-perspective makes possible new human skills and capacities. Cultural Maturity's cognitive reordering produces essential new abilities pertinent to leadership in all parts of our personal and collective lives. To start, this includes the ability to assume a new, more ultimate kind of responsibility—not just for our choices, but also for the truths on which we base our choices. It also includes coming to better tolerate uncertainty and complexity, bringing a new maturity to our relationship to limits, and learning to engage concerns of all sorts in ways that get beyond the either/or polarized assumptions of times past. Each of these new skills and capacities follows from how Integrative Meta-perspective invites us to more consciously and fully engage intelligence's multiplicity.

I will give special attention in these pages to one further new capacity that has particular pertinence in the thinking of Creative Systems Theory. It relates to the importance of learning to think contextually. In a culturally mature reality, we better see how what is true at one time or place may be very different from what is true at another. We can think of Creative Systems Theory as a detailed framework for understanding context. The theory's various "patterning concepts" become possible because of the way Integrative Meta-perspective draws on the whole of intelligence. Most obviously this is true for what the theory calls Patterning in Time distinctions. CST proposes that understanding any developmental process—including history—in terms of what creates significance requires drawing on the whole of intelligence's multiplicity. (I will go into greater detail in Chapter Two.) But the whole of intelligence's multiplicity is just as critical when it comes to more here-and-now systemic distinctions, what the theory calls Patterning in Space. For example, we see its contribution with the Creative

Systems Personality Typology, the theory's framework for understanding temperament diversity that we will visit briefly in Chapter Five. The typology describes how individuals who choose to become artists, actors, teachers, engineers, scientists, or stockbrokers are different not just because their interests differ, but also because their cognitive structures reflect different preferences and balances within intelligence's creative multiplicity.

There is a final, more conceptual way that more fully engaging intelligence's multiplicity adds to understanding in our time. Appreciating intelligence's multiple aspects makes possible more dynamic and encompassing frameworks for understanding such as what we find with Creative Systems Theory. The theory has its basis in a new Fundamental Organizing Concept, a new kind of basic underlying principle.[8] With the rationality-based understandings of Modern Age belief, the Fundamental Organizing Concept was the idea that reality works like a great machine. But machine-model worldviews confront a major obstacle when it comes to human systems. We are not machines. Creative Systems Theory's creative framing of truth in human systems offers a way of thinking that puts the dynamic, living nature of who we are and how we understand at the forefront. That it is able to succeed at this essential task is a product of the way it draws on the whole of intelligence's creative multiplicity. I do not make Creative Systems Theory's particular formulations some last word. But I am comfortable with the assertion that any kind of conceptual framework able to help us going forward must in a similar way draw consciously on the whole of intelligence—and at least a bit appreciate intelligence's generative workings.[9]

---

8 See Charles. M. Johnston, MD, *Insight: Creative Systems Theory's Radical New Picture of Human Possibility*, ICD Press, 2022.

9 Creative Systems Theory not only provides a new Fundamental Organizing Concept for today, its creative framing of history lets us map the Fundamental Organizing Concepts of each

The Dilemma of Trajectory and Intelligence's Multiplicity

An even more radical multiple intelligence–related claim puts an exclamation point on our task with this book. I will propose that if we fail at realizing a new more mature relationship to intelligence's multiplicity, we may well be doomed. An essential quandary highlighted by Creative Systems Theory, what it calls the Dilemma of Trajectory, helps clarify this observation which might seem excessive. The Dilemma of Trajectory makes something at least similar to what the concept of Cultural Maturity suggests inescapably necessary.

We can represent the Dilemma of Trajectory in a simple way using the language of polarity. Each stage in culture to this point has been defined by greater distinction between polar opposites and a greater emphasis on difference more generally. (In tribal times, connectedness to nature and tribe was primary; today it is materiality and individuality that prevails.) But we can also frame the Dilemma of Trajectory in terms of intelligence's multiplicity. We've evolved from times in which the more creatively germinal aspects of intelligence—the body and the imagination—most informed experience (to be part of a tribe is to know those tribal dances and related rituals) to times in which the rational—with a limited contribution from the emotional—holds the much larger influence (enter the Age of Reason). And alternatively, we can describe this evolution using a more general language drawn from the study of myth. Culture's story has taken us from times in which archetypally feminine influences ruled to times in which the archetypally masculine is much more the defining presence.

With our time, this organizing trajectory has reached an extreme. Truth has come to be defined almost exclusively by difference (for example, with how we view objective and subjective as wholly separate worlds), we equate rationality with understanding, and extreme archetypally masculine

---

major chapter in culture's story.

values prevail (such as those of the marketplace or of science). The Dilemma of Trajectory alerts us to how going further in this direction would not benefit us. Indeed, there is an important sense in which going forward as we have really stops being an option. We would not do well if we lost what remaining connection we have with nature, our bodies, or the more receptive aspects of experience that form the basis of human relationship. Proceeding further in this direction would alienate us irretrievably from aspects of who we are that are essential to being human.

So what are we to do? We could go back—a proposal at least implied in certain kinds of social advocacy. But going back is not any more likely to get us where we need to go. Unless there is a further option, the human experiment could be at a conclusion. By reconciling the Dilemma of Trajectory, Integrative Meta-perspective and the more conscious relationship to intelligence's creative multiplicity that it provides offers a possible way forward. And it is a way forward that points toward an essential kind of human realization and fulfillment.

A related Creative Systems Theory concept sheds further light on the importance of a more engaged relationship to intelligence's multiplicity in our times. We will return for a closer look in Chapter Five. It relates to an observation that could seem to prove the concept of Cultural Maturity wrong. A lot that we see in today's world might appear to be almost the opposite of what the concept predicts—for example, increasing political and social polarization, widespread denial with regard to essential limits-related challenges such as climate change and the extinction of species, and today's growing rates of suicide, addiction, and gun violence. Given that we find so much in contemporary human behavior that can seem rather ludicrous, it can be hard to believe that getting wiser as a species is a possibility.

It may not be. But much of what we encounter is in fact consistent with what we would expect to find as we engage Cultural Maturity's demands. Creative Systems Theory describes how our times should be characterized not just by new possibility, but also by distorted ways of thinking. It calls this particular kind of ludicrousness Transitional Absurdity. The important recognition at this point is that Integrative Meta-perspective, and in particular how it brings the possibility of engaging the whole of human intelligence with a new completeness, not only reconciles the Dilemma of Trajectory, it provides the necessary antidote to today's Transitional Absurdities.

CHAPTER TWO

A Glimpse Into the Role of Intelligence's Multiplicity in Making Us Who We Are

I've made reference to how Howard Gardner's writings about multiple intelligences are currently the most recognized. In his 1983 book *Frames of Mind*, he postulates seven intelligence modalities: musical-rhythmic and harmonic, visual-spatial, linguistic-verbal, logical-mathematical, bodily-kinesthetic, interpersonal, and intrapersonal (to which he later suggested adding naturalistic and existential).[1] His work has been criticized by mainstream psychology for its lack of empirical evidence and for its dependence on subjective judgement. But many people, particularly in the field of education, have found it of value for helping us begin to think in more multifaceted ways about intelligence. It has contributed important insights to the debate about expanding how we think about intelligence beyond traditional IQ measures.

I applaud Gardner's contribution. Where it stops short, as I see things, doesn't have so much to do with its dependence on subjective judgement. Indeed, I might argue that it doesn't go far enough in that regard. Rather, it is limited by its observations' lack of depth and nuance. Intelligence's multiple aspects are described only in terms of the

---

1 Howard Gardner, *Frames of Mind: The Theory of Multiple Intelligences*, Basic Books, 2011.

most surface, behavioral characteristics. Creative Systems Theory's more systemic perspective for delineating intelligence's multiplicity attempts to get directly at how our different ways of knowing order experience. The result is a framework that engages intelligences deeply not just in terms of particulars but also at the level of purpose. We also get a framework that is specifically integrative in the sense of helping us understand how our various ways of knowing work together to make us who we are.

Creative Systems Theory's approach starts with the observation that our toolmaking, meaning-making nature means that human intelligence must at least effectively support formative process. The theory then goes on to describe how human intelligence is specifically structured for this task. It notes how we are the uniquely creative creatures that we are not just because we are conscious, but because of the particular ways in which the various aspects of our intelligence work—and how they work together. It describes how our various intelligences relate in specifically creative ways. And it delineates how different ways of knowing, and different relationships between ways of knowing, predominate at specific times in any human change processes. It ties the underlying structures of intelligence to patterns we see in how human systems change—thereby both helping us better understand change and hinting at the possibility that we might better predict change.

Creative Systems Theory and Intelligence's Multiplicity

Creative Systems Theory identifies four basic types of intelligence. For ease of conversation, we can refer to them as the intelligences of the body, the imagination, the emotions, and the intellect (though the theory uses the fancier language that I've included in Figure 2-1). The theory proposes that these different ways of knowing represent not just diverse approaches to processing information, but the windows through which we make sense of our worlds. And, more than this, they represent the formative tendencies that lead us to shape our worlds in the ways that we do.

The theory describes how our various modes of intelligence, juxtaposed like colors on a color wheel, function together as formative process's mechanism. That wheel, like the wheel of a car or a Ferris wheel, is continually turning, continually in motion. The way the various facets of intelligence juxtapose makes change, and specifically purposeful change, inherent to our natures.

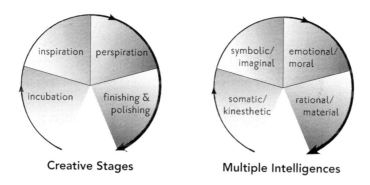

Fig. 2-1. Formative Process and Intelligence

Let's look a bit more closely, starting with a simple creative act.

With creativity's initial, "incubation" stage, a person's sense of what they are going to create will be murky at best. The dominant intelligence here is the kinesthetic, body intelligence if you will. It is like I am pregnant, but don't yet know with quite what. What I do know takes the form of "inklings" and faint "glimmerings," inner sensings.

With creativity's "inspiration" stage—where new form first becomes visible—the dominant intelligence is the imaginal, that which most defines art, myth, and the let's-pretend world of young children. The products of this period in the creative process may appear suddenly—Archimedes's "eureka"—or they may come more subtly and gradually.

During creativity's "perspiration" stage—where the hard work of the creative takes place—the dominant intelligence is different still, more emotional and visceral—the intelligence of heart and guts. It is here that we confront the more focused tasks of finding the right approach and engaging the most effective means of expression.

With creativity's "finishing and polishing" stage, rational intelligence comes to have the more dominant role. This period is more conscious and gives greater attention to aesthetic precision than the periods previous. It is also more concerned with audience and outcome. It brings final focus to the creative work, offers the clarity of thought and nuances of style needed for effective communication.

We might easily think the creative work to be complete at this point, but in fact we are at best half done. We have yet to engage the dynamics that Creative Systems Theory calls Creative Integration. Think of it as creativity's "seasoning" stage. With creative process's second half, we step back from the work and understand it with new perspective. We become more able to appreciate the relationship of the work to its creative contexts, to ourselves, and to the time and place in which it was created. And specifically with regard to intelligence, we come to use our diverse ways of knowing more consciously together. We become able to apply our intelligences in various combinations and balances as time and situation warrant, and through this to engage the work as a whole and ourselves as a whole in relationship to it.

I've noted Creative Systems Theory's essential observation that we see a similar evolving relationship between cognitive sensibilities with formative processes of all sorts. This is the case with any act of innovation, with personal psychological development, with the growth of a relationship or an organization, and with culture and its evolution. A brief summary:

We find the same bodily intelligence that orders creative "incubation" playing a particularly prominent role in the infant's rhythmic world of movement, touch, and taste. The realities of early tribal cultures also draw deeply on body sensibilities. Truth in tribal societies is synonymous with the rhythms of nature and, through dance, song, story, and drumbeat, with the body of the tribe.

In a similar way, we find the same imaginal intelligence that we saw ordering creative "inspiration" taking preeminence in the play-centered world of the young child. We also hear its voice with particular strength in early civilizations—such as in ancient Greece or Egypt, with the Incas and Aztecs in the Americas, or in the classical East—with their mythic pantheons and great symbolic tales.

Again, in a related way, we find the same emotional and moral intelligence that orders creative "perspiration" occupying center stage in adolescence with its deepening passions and pivotal struggles for identity. It can be felt with particular strength also in the beliefs and values of the European Middle Ages, times marked by feudal struggle and ardent moral conviction (and, today, in places where struggle and conflict seem to be forever recurring).

And we find the same rational intelligence that comes forward for the "finishing and polishing" tasks of creativity taking new prominence in young adulthood, as we strive to create our unique place in the world of adult expectations. This more refined and refining aspect of intelligence stepped to the fore culturally with the Renaissance and the Age of Reason and, in the West, has held sway into modern times.

Finally, and of particular pertinence to the concept of Cultural Maturity, we find the same more consciously integrative relationship to intelligence that we see in the "seasoning" stage of a creative act ordering the unique developmental capacities—the wisdom—of a lifetime's second half. We can also often see this same more integrative relationship with intelligence just beneath the surface with cultural advances that have transformed understanding through the last century.

We associate the Age of Reason with Descartes's assertion that "I think, therefore I am." We could make a parallel assertion for each of these other cultural stages: "I am embodied, therefore I am"; "I imagine, therefore I am"; "I am a moral being, therefore I am"; and, if the concept of Cultural Maturity is accurate, "I understand maturely and systemically—with the whole of myself—therefore I am." Cultural Maturity proposes that the discussion you have just read about intelligence's creative workings has been possible because such consciously integrative dynamics are reordering how we think and perceive.

Intelligence and Today's Crisis of Purpose

In the previous chapter, I briefly addressed some of the reasons that a more conscious engagement with the whole of intelligence has become essential. I promised to return for a closer look at one with a particularly immediate kind of significance—the need to address today's Crisis of Purpose. I associate many of the most troubling concerns of our time—such as growing rates of anxiety, depression, and suicide, and the addiction epidemic—with this Crisis of Purpose. Too often in our time people lack a guiding narrative sufficiently compelling to take them forward.

I introduced my short book *Hope and the Future: Confronting Today's Crisis of Purpose* with a story that highlights this easily unsettling circumstance.[2] It involved therapy with a young man who had attempted to hang himself. It became strikingly clear in our work together that the hopelessness he felt was only in limited ways personal. It was more about the state of the world. He described having a hard time thinking of a future he would want to be a part

---

2 Charles M. Johnston, MD, *Hope and the Future: Confronting Today's Crisis of Purpose*, ICD Press, 2016.

of. Work with the young man eventually came down to exploring how he could conceive of the future in a way that for him became purposeful. In Chapter Three, I will touch briefly on the particular approach I used for doing this. For now, the important recognitions are that the methodology that got us there directly supported culturally mature understanding and drew on the whole of intelligence.

Some general observations help make the connection with intelligence's multiple aspects. Reengaging emotional intelligence along with the rational helped him get beyond the looking-out-for-number-one assumptions of mass material culture and more deeply appreciate the role of relationship in his life. Reengaging imaginal intelligence with its language of image, myth, and metaphor helped him come to better grasp existence as generative and creative. And reengaging body intelligence helped him connect more deeply with experience at its most immediate and with the ground of his being. By more consciously engaging the whole of himself, he began to tap into the new kind of guiding reality that the concept of Cultural Maturity describes, even though he has no overt knowledge of such a concept.

Reflecting on the mechanics of addiction helps fill out this kind of recognition. The opioid epidemic provides a particularly striking illustration of today's Crisis of Purpose. As a therapist, I would prefer that there was a simple approach—psychotherapeutic or pharmacological—that would reliably provide an antidote. And as someone who advises on public policy, I similarly wish that there was some simple law or policy that would take care of things. In fact, opioid addiction all too often proves impervious to treatment. And neither harsher penalties nor removing penalties and spending more money on treatment seem to greatly influence the numbers. I've reluctantly come to the conclusion that any solution that will have major effect in the long term must be tied to the kinds of changes I describe with the concept of Cultural Maturity. Given that we can't just will those changes, that is not good news as far as the addiction crisis. But appreciating where answers ultimately lie at least supports asking the right questions and helps us not go off in directions that easily do more harm than good.

The opioid epidemic represents only one example of addictive dynamics in our time. The addicting substance can as well be food with today's obesity crisis, products to buy with the material excesses of mass popular culture, or the artificial stimulation in the name of meaning so common in our high-tech world. Addicting substances work by providing false substitutes for real fulfillment. By activating brain centers tied to feelings like pleasure, power, excitement, or the spiritual, they generate the experience of meaning without requiring the vulnerability and commitment needed for the real thing.[3] I think of our current vulnerability to addiction as a key example of Transitional Absurdity.

In my experience, therapy that is successful with addiction necessarily achieves something similar to what I described in working with my client who attempted to hang himself. It somehow helps the person get in touch with real meaning in their lives (and also to find the courage to shape their lives in ways that support it). Success happens when the person gets to the place where the real thing becomes so important to them that they will not accept imposters. Increasingly, as with my suicidal client, the real thing needs to be not just personal; it needs to in some way relate to purpose in a larger sense. And more often than not, it will be tied in some way to the specific larger kind of purpose that becomes understandable only with Cultural Maturity's cognitive reordering. Where this is the

---

3 In an experiment often described in psychology classes to teach about addiction, wires are run from excitement centers in a rat's brain to a depressible pedal in its cage. After the rat discovers the pedal, he pushes it with ever greater frequency, in the end abandoning other activities including eating, and dies.

case, a deeper connecting with the whole of intelligence's multiplicity will necessarily play a role in realizing purpose in this more complete sense.

Human Advancement and Intelligence's Multiplicity

Recognizing the Crisis of Purpose felt by so many people individually today brings attention to a pivotal task that today confronts us more collectively. Our times are requiring us to revisit our ideas about what constitutes advancement—to fundamentally rethink wealth and progress. Again, the ability to more deeply engage intelligence's creative multiplicity is critical to success in doing so. With our Modern Age, we have come to define advancement almost exclusively in terms of invention and material growth—measures that reflect rational intelligence values. Integrative Meta-perspective's deeper engagement with the whole of intelligence offers that we might think about advancement in more systemic and complete ways.

When I want to help people address the advancement question, I will often first ask them to talk to me about what creates wealth in their individual lives. Most people mention money, but they also tend to recognize that beyond a certain point money stops being significant in the same sense. Invention, too, most always has a place—people like their gadgets. But most people appreciate that other things are ultimately as important—or often much more important: one's family, one's friends, one's community, one's felt relationship with nature, one's health, one's creative and intellectual pursuits.

People doing this exercise are often surprised to find that a significant mismatch exists between what they have described as most important for a rich life and many of their day-to-day choices. I may joke with the person as they confront this mismatch, pointing out—only partly tongue in cheek—that such discrepancy would seem to be almost the definition of insanity. When arrived at in therapy, this kind of recognition can result in people making major life changes.

If the person has interest in the larger, cultural-level question, I may then engage them in the same kind of inquiry with regard to how collectively we define wealth and progress. People tend to come up with lists that are very similar, both in being more encompassing and in better reflecting basic needs. The fact that current world priorities reflect a related kind of mismatch becomes hard to escape. Too often today we apply an outmoded definition of advancement that excludes much that is in fact most important to us. And just as we appropriately think of individuals who make choices that are not in keeping with what they find most significant as deranged, the implications are huge. With the Dilemma of Trajectory, we see how continuing to take our Modern Age definition beyond its timeliness can only leave us ever more distanced from much that most ultimately matters to us.

Rethinking wealth and progress is ultimately about much more than just finding more sustainable measures. It is about a next chapter in how we think about "more." Getting there requires drawing on the whole of who we are—in particular, the whole of intelligence's multiplicity. While our Modern Age measures drew almost exclusively on rational/material intelligence, our new measures necessarily also access other intelligences, and not just as decoration, but as central contributors to any reasonable conclusion. If we are to effectively include the importance of human relationship in our measures, we need the contribution of emotional intelligence. If we are to include the value of life imbued with creativity and inspiration, imaginal intelligence must similarly have a seat at the table. And if we are to include the renewed valuing of nature (or our own deep nature) required for any deeply engaged future, we also need the contribution of body intelligence.

It is important to recognize how more complete definitions of progress will be necessary not just if we are to conceive of advancement as a whole usefully, but also if we are to effectively engage almost any more specific critical task ahead for the species. Certainly, measures that follow from a more encompassing definition will be required if we are to successfully assess the benefits and risks of new technologies. More systemic yardsticks will be needed if we are to effectively determine what we are to call benefit. They will similarly be critical if we are to make good environmental decisions. It is only through such more complete measures that we can appreciate how impoverished further environmental destruction would leave us. And a more mature and systemic definition for wealth and progress will clearly also be necessary if we are to effectively address the ever-widening gap between the world's haves and have-nots. Ask about benefit more consciously and we begin to better recognize not just how such disparities are ethically troubling, but how they risk destabilizing societies and putting everyone's well-being in peril. In each case, the ability to make choices wisely depends on the ability to engage and draw on the whole of intelligence's rich and creative multiplicity.

CHAPTER THREE

A Closer Look at Intelligence's Multiplicity

Since the notion that intelligence has multiple aspects can be foreign to usual understanding—and the implications are so pivotal—it is worth taking the time to look at each of the four kinds of intelligence that I've made reference to more closely. Here I'll start by noting some of the figures from psychiatry and psychology who have most contributed to understanding each of them. I'll then offer more detailed descriptions. And finally, I'll address a couple more nuanced topics that help fill out the importance of drawing with real depth and detail on what each kind of intelligence potentially contributes—first, how particular intelligences manifest in different ways in different contexts, and second, how, while each intelligence helps us get at the truth, each can also be used to lie and deceive.

Intelligence's Multiplicity and the Twentieth-Century Evolution of Psychiatry and Psychology

One of the things that first drew me to become a psychiatrist was the way in which key figures in the evolution of psychiatry and psychology had brought attention to aspects of intelligence's workings that with modern times we have put at arm's length. We could include Sigmund Freud's early highlighting of unconscious processes in this regard, but his reference was to unconscious forces more generally, rather than to specific ways of knowing. He also saw the unconscious more as a repository for repressed thoughts and feelings than something generative.

Later figures more specifically brought attention to particular ways of knowing. Indeed, where their work confronted limitations, it was often because they gave some particular intelligence a monopoly on truth rather than thinking of it as an aspect of cognition's larger picture. For the nonrational aspects of intelligence, I think most immediately of Wilhelm Reich for the psychology of the body,[1] Carl Jung for the imaginal world of myth and symbol,[2] and for the more emotional, the early figures of humanistic psychology such as Carl Rogers,[3] Rollo May, and Virginia Satir. The non-rational more generally got further attention at bit later with transpersonal psychology, including the thinking of Abraham Maslow[4] and others of more spiritual inclination.

In recent years, psychological practice has turned more to rationalistic interpretations of the psychological and to more mechanistic methodologies. Cognitive behavioral therapy, with its origins in the thinking of Aaron Beck, represents one example.[5] Cognitive behavioral therapy involves changing how people think to improve how they feel. Because it is easy to grasp rationally and most in keeping with Modern Age sensibilities, it is not surprising that it is now the most frequently taught approach in clinical settings. But it leaves out much of what is most important in making us who we are as purposeful beings.

---

1 Wilhelm Reich, *The Function of the Orgasm*, Farrar, Straus & Giroux, 1986. This thread continued with the neo-Reichian thinking of people like Alexander Lowen and my early mentor, Stanley Keleman.

2 Carl Jung, *Man and His Symbols*, Dell, 1968.

3 Carl Rogers, *On Becoming a Person*, Harper Collins, 1995.

4 Abraham Maslow, *Toward a Psychology of Being*, Wilder, 2011.

5 Aaron Beck, *Cognitive Therapy and the Emotional Disorders*, Plume, 1979.

There can be debate in psychological circles between people who use methods that work at a more surface, behavioral level and those who use approaches that engage more deeply. It often pits those who advocate for addressing issues in the here and now against those who attempt to get at root causes through probing a person's history. I consider each kind of approach to be limited. I tend to make use of methodologies that work in the present but that very specifically involve a deep engagement with people's diverse ways of knowing (a topic of the next chapter).

Psychiatry and psychology are not the only fields where nonrational aspects of intelligence have been given newly conscious attention in the last century. We also find contributions from the performing arts.[6] And we find insights from the world of medicine that address mind-body interactions in disease and important ways in which the body is intelligent, from how the endocrine system recognizes pathogens to how much more our gut does than just process our dinners. But here our focus will be with Creative Systems Theory's particular approach to understanding intelligence's multiplicity. The theory is unusual in the depth it brings to understanding knowing's various aspects. And it is unique in the picture it presents of how the various aspects of intelligence work together to make us the audaciously inventive and constantly reflective creatures that we are.

Four Primary Ways of Knowing

Let's take a closer look at the four primary intelligences that Creative Systems Theory identifies. I've noted that the theory uses more formal language when describing body,

---

6 With dance, I think in particular of the work of Rudolf Laban (Rudolf Laban, "Meister und Werk in der Tanzkunst," *Deutsche Tanzzeitschrift*, May 1936), and with voice and theater the contribution of F.M. Alexander (F.M. Alexander, *The Use of the Self*, Orion, 1932).

imaginal, emotional, and rational ways of knowing. Here I will apply this more formal terminology: somatic/kinesthetic intelligence, symbolic/imaginal intelligence, emotional/moral intelligence, and rational/material intelligence. This more filled-out language helps point toward the complexity of experience that each different kind of intelligence ultimately reflects.

Somatic/Kinesthetic Intelligence

God guard me from those thoughts men think
In the mind alone:
He that sings a lasting song
Thinks in a marrow-bone.
              —William Butler Yeats

The intelligence of the body is the aspect of knowing that we tend to be least consciously in touch with in our time. Certainly it is the most difficult to give expression to in words. Many people would not immediately think of it as intelligence. But arguably, it provides the foundation on which every other aspect of intelligence rests.

We all draw on body intelligence as a primary way of knowing as infants. And body intelligence necessarily has a central role with erotic and aesthetic experience throughout our lives. Of particular pertinence to this book's reflections, body intelligence has defining significance in the germinal beginnings of any creative/development dynamic. The earliest knowing in any life process is bodily knowing.

Body with this most germinal stage in creation is very different from the body as we conceive of it through the isolated and isolating eye of Modern Age understanding. It is much more than simply sensation; also much more than simply anatomy and physiology; and more than one side of an either/or: body versus mind, or body versus spirit. In the first stage of formativeness, body intelligence is who we are. It is how we organize our experience of both ourselves and our world.

People who are dancers, athletes, cooks, or practitioners of certain healing arts such as physical therapy and massage draw deeply on the intelligence of the body. So do sculptors (body intelligence is strong in my makeup) and musicians, particularly where the rhythmic aspect of musical aesthetic has prominence. Body intelligence can also play a strong role with people who work in the trades—as with carpentry or plumbing. And activities we describe as crafts—such as knitting or sewing—often directly depend on bodily sensibilities.

While we don't tend to give body intelligence in its less obviously physical manifestations much status in formal thought, it has a central place in the concrete experience of our lives. For example, if you say you love someone and you are asked how you know, eventually you will begin to talk in the language of the body. You know you feel love because when you are with the person you care about, your "heart" opens—there is a warm expanding in the area of the chest. This experienced "heart" cannot be found by dissection. But it is undeniably very real, very close to what is most essential in us.

Bodily experience in this sense, while often unconscious, can take colorful expression in our figures of speech.[7] We speak of feeling "moved" or "touched," of being "beside ourselves," or feeling that something is "over our heads." And if we take the time, a lot of this sort of experience is available to us consciously. As a simple example, if I pay attention, I recognize that I feel my bodily connection with different people in quite different ways. With one person I may feel it most as a sense of fullness and solidity in my belly or shoulders. With another, I may know it most as a sense of animation in my eyes and face, or erotic arousal in my genitals. With certain people, I feel our meeting very close to the core

---

7 Note that the phrase "figure of speech" could be thought of as a reference to bodily knowing.

of my body; with others, the bodily experience of meeting may feel much more peripheral, more "superficial."[8]

When I want to get in touch with bodily knowing, there are particular things I can do. I can simply be aware in my flesh. I can also be more receptive in the world—my senses are what I am receptive with. When I want to tap the deep generative levels of this kind of knowing, I may soak in a warm bath or take a walk in some quiet place.

In Chapter Six, I will offer a more focused look at body intelligence, in particular, how our experience of the body is different depending on when in developmental processes we look and also for people with different personality styles. For now, some historical quotes help fill out how the body lives not just as experience, but as a way of knowing:

> The words of language do not seem to play a role in my mech-
> anisms of thought ...the elements are, in my case, of visual
> and some of muscular type. Conventional words [come in]...
> a secondary stage....
> > —Albert Einstein

> Yes, Yes
> that's what
> I always wanted, to return
> to the body
> where I was born.
> > —Allen Ginsberg

> Our most sacred convictions, the unchanging elements in our
> supreme values, are judgments of the muscles.
> > —Friedrich Nietzsche

---

8 We commonly think of the word "superficial" as disparaging, but here I use it only to refer to the more surface layers of body experience. Chapter Five's look at the Creative Systems Personality Typology and Chapter Six's deeper look at body experience will help clarify this key distinction.

The body never lies.
        —Martha Graham

*... the soul is not more than the body... and the body is not
more than the soul.*
        —Walt Whitman

It don't mean a thing, if it ain't got that swing.
        —Duke Ellington

Symbolic/Imaginal Intelligence

Dreams are the true interpreter of our inclinations.
        —Michel de Montaigne

While the imaginal tends to be better recognized in our time as a way of knowing than body intelligence, in most contexts it is similarly given secondary status. Activities that draw deeply on it tend to be thought of as decoration to life's more serious pursuits. In fact, it plays a central role in making anyone's life full and vital.

Symbolic/imaginal intelligence is the vehicle of myth, dream, metaphor, and much in artistic expression. Like the intelligence of the body, it speaks from close to the beginnings of things, but not quite so close. When a storyteller utters the words, "Once upon a time...," it is more than simple convention. The words are a bidding to remember an essential kind of magic.

The imaginal gives us the period in formative process that we most associate with things creative. Imaginal/mythic intelligence organizes reality in the stage of inspiration, that critical time when bubblings from the dream work of the unconscious give us our first visible sense of what is asking to become. The symbolic is both the organizing truth and the chief mode of expression as new possibility first makes itself felt. The "aha" stage in any life process speaks the language of symbolic/imaginal intelligence.

Symbolic/imaginal intelligence, taking expression as myth, serves as truth's most direct expression with culture's early rise. Joseph Campbell described the mythic aspect of the imaginal this way in his book *Myths to Live By*: "It would not be too much to say that myth is the secret opening through which the inexhaustible energies of the cosmos pour into human cultural manifestation. Religion, philosophies, social forms of primitive and historic man, prime discoveries in science and technology, the very dreams that blister sleep boil up from the basic magic ring of myth."[9] All of us draw strongly on symbolic/imaginal intelligence during childhood irrespective of our personality style. The child's work happens in a world of let's pretend. And we all engage this aspect of knowing throughout our lives with humor and at any time that we ponder new possibilities.

People who become visual artists, inventors, visionary writers, or comedians tend to have particular facility with imaginal intelligence. This is also the case with many musicians, particularly where improvisation is involved. Given how symbolic/imaginal intelligence orders the childhood world of make-believe, it is not surprising that we also commonly find imaginal intelligence having a central presence in the personalities of people who work with young children (though particularly with very young children, body intelligence can have as strong a place; and with teachers, emotional intelligence is often strongest). Today, we also often find imaginal/mythic intelligence playing a strong role in the inventions of high-tech, particular with its early innovators.

What do we do if we want to get in touch with symbolic/imaginal intelligence? We ponder and think playfully. We laugh. We try something we have never done before, particularly something like painting or making music. We let the moment surprise us. If we are problem solving, we may brainstorm, being sure to make room for the most unexpected of possible solutions. We may visit an art museum or take time to write down our dreams.

---

9 Joseph Campbell, *Myths to Live By*, Penguin, 1993.

A few historical quotes:

I'll play it first, and tell you what it is later.
                    —Miles Davis

When time and waiting need split the ancient egg, out stepped
Love the first born, fire in his eyes, wearing both sexes, glori-
ous Eros.
                    —Orphic Cosmogony

from spiralling ecstatically this
proud nowhere of earth's most prodigious night blossoms a
newborn babe.

… not one heartbeat of this child; nor shall ever prevail a
million questionings
against the silence of her mother's smile —whose only secret
all creation sings.
                    —e.e. cummings

Out of chaos the imagination frames a thing of beauty.
                    —John Livingston Lowes

If you bring forth what is within you,
what you bring forth will save you.
If you do not bring forth what is within you,
what you do not bring forth will destroy you.
                    —Gnostic Gospels (Gospel of Thomas 14.29-33)

Emotional/Moral intelligence

I am wealthy in my friends.
                    — Shakespeare

Emotional intelligence is more familiar to us in our
time than the previous two. It is one step closer to the
rational sensibilities that today most hold sway. But it

is only recently that people have begun to give it status as intelligence (and many people would still not go that far). Historically, it is the aspect of intelligence that we have most associated with the subjective and placed opposite to "real" truth. With Modern Age thought, we specifically cleansed the emotions from our theoretical formulations so that our ideas would have the rigor needed for arm's-length understanding.

People with large amounts of emotional/moral intelligence in their makeup often become teachers, ministers, social workers, police officers, or writers of fiction (where character and relationships are primary). We also find emotional intelligence central in any setting where family and community values play a large role. We all draw on emotional/moral intelligence in our friendships. We also do so when making moral choices. When emotional intelligence is preeminent, life is imbued with a visceral immediacy, and often it is relationship as much as ourselves that holds our attention. Emotional/moral intelligence is what bonds soldiers together in battle. It is also what has parents love their children even when their children are not being particularly lovable. We find it strongly present wherever commitment and perseverance are valued.

With regard to this book's particular framing of intelligence, its role comes most to the fore with the "perspiration" stage of any formation process. In our individual lifetimes, emotional/moral intelligence makes its presence felt with particular strength in the fervencies and allegiances of adolescence. It similarly stood forefront with the crusading ardency and codes of honor and chivalry of the Middle Ages. And we see it in the courage to struggle and the devoted commitment—the "heart and guts"—necessary to take any personal experience of creative inspiration into manifest form.

The emotional as we know it in our current stage in culture has become only a faint vestige of the feeling dimension at its full grandeur as a primary organizing reality. The fact that somehow we must more deeply engage this aspect of ourselves and do so as an integral part of how we understand truth becomes obvious if we examine the issues that now confront us as a species. Solving the dilemmas of our future will require a keen sensitivity to the fact of human relationship and deep levels of personal integrity and ethical responsibility. It is our emotional selves that most appreciate and understand these sorts of concerns.

If we want to get in touch with this aspect of intelligence, we need only ask ourselves what we most deeply care about in any situation. We can also observe our friendships and appreciate what it is that they add to our lives. We can observe ourselves when rooting for our favorite sports team. Or we can simply note what it feels like when we really put our hearts into anything.[10]

A few historical quotes:

The perception of beauty is a moral test.
                    —Henry David Thoreau

After experiencing a desire to invent a particular thing, I may go on for months or years with the idea in the back of my head. Whenever I feel like it, I roam around in

---

10 The phrase "emotional intelligence" tends to be associated these days with the writing of psychologist Daniel Goleman. (Daniel Goleman, *Emotional Intelligence*, Bantam Books, 1995.) The notion, in fact, has a long history, certainly back to the eighteenth-century romantics, and ultimately back much further. Goleman's work has made a valuable contribution, but in the end it divides intelligence into the simple polarity of rational versus emotional. And in keeping with Golman's academic and cognitive science background, his interpretation of the emotional aspect of our cognitive complexity tends to put greatest emphasis on the work and educational competence side of emotional intelligence. In his words, emotional intelligence includes "self-control, zeal, persistence, and the ability to motivate oneself." A creative framing of emotional intelligence incorporates these aspects, but it also includes emotional intelligence's deeper, more intimate, and more specifically generative dimensions.

my imagination and think about the problem without any
deliberate concentration ... then follows a period of direct
effort.
                    —Nikola Tesla

Love one another, but make not a bond of love...
Fill each other's cup, but drink not from one cup ...
Give your hearts, but not into each other's keeping.
                    —Kahlil Gibran

I never met my husband till the day I married him, but it was
a love match till the day he died. And why shouldn't it be for
he was a fine big man.
                    —Peig Sayers (*An Old Woman's Reflections—*
from Her Life on the Blasket Islands off Ireland's West Coast)

Sin is not hurtful because it is forbidden, it is forbidden be-
cause it is hurtful.
                    —Benjamin Franklin

Rational/Material Intelligence

I wish you to consider, finally that all the functions which
I attribute to this machine, such as...waking and sleeping;
the reception of light, sounds, odors..., the impression of
ideas in the memory; the inferior movements of the appe-
tites and passions...; I desire, I say, that you consider that
these functions occur naturally in this machine solely by
the disposition of its organs, not less than the movements
of a clock.
                    —René Descartes, *Discourse on Method*

Rational/material intelligence is the intelligence of syl-
logistic logic—if A, then B, then C. In today's world, we
tend to assume it defines intelligence. Rational/material
intelligence is the larger part of what we measure with IQ
tests and most engage and reward with formal education.

We tend to equate it with being objective and make it an opposite to the other more "subjective" sensibilities.

We all draw on rational/material intelligence in solving problems. And very often it is the intelligence that gets the credit when we make choices, even when other intelligences have in fact played the larger role. When we tell someone what we think about something, we are most likely to talk in the language of rational/material intelligence.

Where rational intelligence predominates in a person's makeup, they might commonly become professors, writers of nonfiction, businesspeople, journalists, scientists, or accountants. Doctors and political leaders also need to draw strongly on rational intelligence, but in each case the people skills that come with emotional intelligence must also play a significant role if they are to be effective.

As far as rational/material intelligence's role in formative process, it comes most strongly to the fore with the period of finishing and polishing. We find it then dominant with any specifically creative endeavor. With individual psychological development, it orders adult understanding. And in modern times, it represents the kind of cognitive processing that gave us Enlightenment thought and Modern Age institutions.

That we specifically elevate the rational in modern culture doesn't mean that rational processing doesn't have an important place in the cognitive processes of earlier cultural times. But depending on the cultural stage, the underlying premises of our "logic" will have their roots in that time's often decidedly nonrational organizing sensibilities. With earliest times, for example, rationality will reflect underlying animistic (body intelligence) assumptions. Imagine two cave dwellers discussing the various creatures depicted on a cave wall.

With Modern Age culture, the underlying premises of our logical assertions come to have their roots as well in rational/material assumptions. Rationality is allied with awareness, and together with it becomes, in effect, final truth. We come to view causality increasingly in terms of actions and their concomitant reactions, identity in terms of what we think, and wealth and progress almost exclusively in terms of material acquisition and technological innovation.

We tend to be most familiar with what it takes to get in touch with the rational aspect of intelligence, though we may dig in our heels when it comes to the task of applying it clearly. We simply need to think things through. If we want to engage rational/material intelligence even more, we can read some philosophy or serious literature. Or if it is more our inclination, we can ponder the latest insights from science or mathematics.

> *Science is nothing but trained and organized common sense.*
> —T.H. Huxley

> *Well, pray if you like, only you'd do better to use your judgement.*
> —Leo Tolstoy

> *Men prosper or fail, survive or perish, in proportion to the degree of their rationality.*
> —Ayn Rand

> *I think looking back on my own childhood, the fact that so many of the stories I read allowed the possibility of frogs turning into princes, whether that has a sort of insidious effect on rationality, I'm not sure. Perhaps it is something for research.*
> —Richard Dawkins

> *We have almost reached the point where praise of rationality is held to mark a man as an old fogey regrettably surviving from a bygone age.*
> —Bertrand Russell

Beyond One Intelligence/One Stage

This expanded picture of intelligence needs one further recognition if it is to adequately capture intelligence's role in formative process. To keep things simple, for the most part thus far I've spoken as if we can identify each intelligence with a particular creative stage. In fact, each intelligence plays a role at each stage. Specific intelligences do most define understanding with each creative stage, but in a manner similar to what I just suggested for the rational, each of intelligence's multiple aspects also has a part in the workings of each stage, manifesting in a particular and predictable way as an element in the larger sensibility that orders that stage's generative task. We need this further recognition if our thinking is to have any degree of nuance. Here, again, I will focus on this more multilayered reality as it pertains to chapters in culture's developmental story.

While the intelligence of the body is primary in tribal times, body experience certainly remains present with the deeply felt mythic intensities that we find with the early high cultures. And certainly, too, we find it with the deep moral convictions and emotional allegiances of medieval sensibilities. And while body intelligence's role is least explicit in modern times where we tend to think of the body primarily in physical terms, it very much manifests in our sensory worlds, with erotic impulses, and in limited ways with the arts.

We find a related more multifaceted picture with imaginal/symbolic intelligence. The imaginal takes its most dominant expression in "inspiration stage" cultural realities, with their pantheons of gods, elaborate mythic tales, and great richnesses of artistic expression. But while imaginal/symbolic intelligence takes a back seat to bodily knowing in tribal times, it nonetheless has an important role then too, manifesting as animistic imagery with its clear message of inseparability from nature (think of the evocative power of those cave paintings). With "perspiration stage" times in culture, imaginal/symbolic intelligence takes a secondary role to emotional/moral intelligence's now defining presence, but it continues to contribute. Myth's numinosity gives way to the more explicitly moral language of legend (think of the medieval tales of the Knights of the Round Table). And while art ceases to be itself a definer of truth, it continues to serve powerfully as a language for religious sensibility (think of the power of symbol in a medieval cathedral). With "finishing and polishing" stage realities, while we still appreciate imaginal/symbolic intelligence—indeed, with the arts, it can have an elevated presence—increasingly its role becomes more decorative. With more popular expression, it takes the form of fantasy.

We encounter a similarly multifaceted reality with emotional/moral intelligence. Emotional sensibilities play the most defining role in "perspiration stage" times. But the bond a tribesperson feels with nature or with other members of the tribe clearly has emotional aspects. And certainly the inspired symbolic tales of the early high cultures are emotionally evocative. In Modern Age times, anything we would attribute to the humanities as opposed to the sciences or business reflects the emotional as much as the rational. The humanities have less direct influence than their more materially defined complements—and in our time that influence has markedly diminished—but they nonetheless garner respect. The word "sentiment" perhaps best captures this aspect of emotional intelligence.

The chart in Figure 3-1 outlines these relationships. I've indicated the primary intelligences at each stage with an asterisk (*). Finding useful language for these more detailed distinctions can present a challenge, but it is a different kind of challenge than we confront with culturally mature systemic understanding and the task of conceiving in ways that more directly reflect the fact that we are living beings.[11] The challenge here is a product of two factors in

---

11 I've described how a core accomplishment of Creative Systems Theory is that it steps beyond machine models and offers that we might think about human systems in living terms. I've also noted that its success with this accomplishment follows from how Integrative Meta-perspective draws consciously on the whole of who we are as systems. Ideas that are a product of Integrative Meta-perspective, because of all that they necessarily encompass, inherently escape conventional depiction.

CREATIVE LANGUAGES (* = Primary Organizing Language)

The Body	*The Creature Body, the Body as Nature	The Body as Essence, the Body of Ritual, the Spirit or Dream Body	The Visceral/Muscular Body, the Body of "Heart and Guts"	The Physical Body, the Body as Appearance
The Symbolic	Animism – the Symbolic as a Language of Nature	*Myth – the Symbolic as a Language of Ritual and Inspirational Relationship	Legend – the Symbolic as a Language of Moral Order	Fantasy – the Symbolic as a Language of Romanticism and Idealism
The Emotional	Feeling as Harmony with Nature	Feeling as Inspiration, Essence, and Primal Passion	*Feeling as Visceral Emotion	Feeling as Sentiment and Pleasure
The Intellect	Participatory Conciousness	Magical and Aesthetic Thought	The Logic of Right and Wrong	*Rational, Mechanistic Thought

Fig. 3-1. The Multilayered Manifestations of Intelligence's Creative Multiplicity

combination. First is the simple fact that many of these intelligences by their nature tend not to function at the level of language. Second is the way that modern times can leave us estranged from their underlying realities.

Language is particularly tricky with body intelligence, given that it lies furthest from the more verbal parts of our cognitive functioning. We could also call what I've labelled the "creature body" in the chart the body of nature or the organic body. We can think of the "body as essence" alternatively as the ritual body, the energy body, or the inspired body. I often call what I have labeled the "visceral/muscular body" the body of heart and guts. The "physical body" is the body of anatomy and physiology and also the body of sensation and of appearances. Conventional language tends to work better for the remaining intelligences, but we still often need to stretch common usage to get at all that is involved.

Deception and Intelligence's Creative Multiplicity

Just because a person does a better job of drawing on intelligence's multiplicity does not mean that they are always going to get things right. Any intelligence can be deceived. And any intelligence can be used to lie, even (and of particular importance) to oneself.

For example, while getting more in touch with kinesthetic/body intelligence provides one of the best ways to bring greater nuance to our perceptions, this doesn't mean that body intelligence can always be trusted. Martha Graham's claim that "the body never lies" makes a kind of point, but in fact the body lies all the time. Witness the role of deceptive and unhelpful bodily responses with addiction, with obesity, or with how bodily reactions can have us be attracted to people who are not at all good for us.

It is the same with every other aspect of intelligence. Getting more connected to imaginal/mythic intelligence is one of the best ways to enhance creativity and vitality in our lives. But imaginal intelligence when used poorly can have us confuse fantasy and wishful thinking with good judgement. At the extreme, we get the kind of "magical thinking" that is a common symptom with psychosis.

Coming to better know our emotional/moral intelligence makes us more adept interpersonally and helps us more deeply engage with life at the level of values. But emotional intelligence can have us confuse emotional soap opera with real significance. And emotional reactiveness can result in decidedly poor choices, such as when anger erupts into war. Even reactive emotions that feel positive can lead us astray (love, indeed, can be blind). Poet and novelist Margaret Atwood observed of the emotional: "Feelings are real...and they can be plausible explanations for all kinds of behavior. But they are not excuses or justifications. If they were, men who murder their wives because they're feeling cranky that day would never get convicted."

As with each intelligence, rationality at the least fails us when it is applied in isolation, when we make it truth's last word. A central tenet in these reflections has been that much that is ultimately most important to us necessarily escapes rational analysis. There is a sense in which this conclusion applies even to the most rational of endeavors. It turns out that science's assumption that the universe is rationally knowable is, in the end, a "faith claim." And as with each of the other ways of knowing, it is true too that the rational can more specifically deceive. Anyone who has been on a debate team knows that you can use rational argument to support most any conclusion (learning how to do so is much of the exercise with debate). And self-deception when it comes to people's concepts of themselves tends to be more common than not.

On the Nature of Objectivity

An essential outcome with Integrative Meta-perspective's more multilayered picture of intelligence might seem to be a paradox. On one hand, because culturally mature perspective draws on diverse, sometimes conflicting, and often fallible aspects of who we are, its conclusions are going to seem less absolute and once-and-for-all than those we are used to. But at the same time, a person could argue that the result is more objective than what it replaces. Certainly it is more complete. Enlightenment thought might have claimed ultimate objectivity, but this was in fact objectivity of a most limited sort. Besides leaving culture's parental status untouched, it left experience as a whole divided—objective (in the old sense) set opposed to subjective, mind set opposed to body, thoughts set opposed to feelings (and anything else that does not conform to modernity's rationalist/materialist worldview). We cannot ultimately claim to be objective if we have left out half of the evidence. Culturally mature "objectivity" is of a more specifically whole-box-of-crayons sort. While truth in this sense asks more of us, it is what must guide us, both personally and collectively, if our decisions going forward are ultimately to serve us.

CHAPTER FOUR

Experiential Approaches

I've noted that I often use hands-on, experiential methods to help people connect with intelligence's multiple aspects. In the year-long leadership Intensives that I did for many years through the Institute for Creative Development, such approaches played an essential role. We wouldn't dive right in with these experiential approaches at the very beginning. Our focus on the first weekend would be on getting a general sense of what addressing critical issues from the perspective of Cultural Maturity might look like. But very soon I would turn to the role of Cultural Maturity's cognitive reordering in making the needed more systemic understanding possible and to the importance with it of intelligence's creative multiplicity. Experiential approaches would provide direct engagement with intelligence's multiple dimensions.

Here I will provide short versions of some of the exercises that I drew on to help people get more in touch with kinesthetic/body intelligence, imaginal/mythic intelligence, emotional/moral intelligence, and rational/material intelligence. Each exercise I will describe is designed not just to engage that particular aspect of intelligence's creative multiplicity, but to do so in a way that supports Integrative Meta-perspective. I will then briefly introduce the hands-on method that works most reliably to generate and support culturally mature understanding. Much of what makes it work is how directly it draws on intelligence as a whole, not just conceptually, but through the structure of the methodology.

Intelligence Exercises

Somatic/Kinesthetic Intelligence:

If you want to get in touch with bodily experience, you could do some dance moves or some yoga, or lift some weights. But exercises that I applied in the Intensive were designed more specifically to bring attention to the body as a way of knowing. After inviting people to stand up and walk slowly around the room, I would ask participants to be attentive to various parts of their bodies as they moved: the bottoms of their feet, their fingers, the length of their spine, the curve of their thighs, their buttocks, their eyes and foreheads. I would then invite them to let different parts of their bodies lead their movements, to explore what happened if they let their hands (and what their hands most cared about) be in charge—to do a "hand dance," and to really get into it. I would then have people do the same thing letting other parts of the body be in charge—to do a "heart dance," a "buttocks dance," a "sole of the foot dance," a "belly dance," an "ear dance," a "genitals dance," an "eye dance," an "elbow dance." I would suggest that people reflect on where each "dance" took them—the sensory qualities, and beyond that, the values and even worldviews that came with having that part run the show.

This first part of the exercise might take over an hour, with people sometimes stopping and jotting notes to themselves as they went through the progression. Eventually, I would ask questions designed to help deepen recognitions. What had most surprised people in what they experienced? Were there particular body-aspect realities that they found themselves identifying with—others that they felt uncomfortable with? Were there some body-aspect realities that felt in conflict with others? With each bodily aspect, did they notice not only differences in inner experience, but also differences in how they experienced the world around them?

Finally, I would invite people to again move around the room, but now while being consciously attentive simultaneously to all of these various bodily aspects, each with its particular sensory qualities, values, and worldviews. I would ask people to notice if in doing so there were ways that being in themselves now felt different. I would also invite people to look around the room and notice if anything had changed in how they experienced other people or the physical space.

Symbolic/Imaginal Intelligence:

If you want to access the imaginal, you can tell some fairy tales, read some mythology, or perhaps visit an art museum. The approaches I would use to engage imaginal intelligence in the Intensive drew on active imagination/visualization techniques. I would start by having people lie down, close their eyes, and take a few deep breaths. (I might introduce a basic relaxation technique to help deepen the relaxed state.) With one visualization I often used, I would first suggest that people imagine themselves on some kind of journey, real or make-believe. It might be along a pathway, on a river, or flying through the air. Once people had come up with an image, I would then have them look around in the image and notice everything they could. And I would ask questions: What kind of vehicle are you traveling in/on (if any at all)? What is the quality of the movement (fast, bumpy, scary, struggled)? Is there anyone else around (and if so, how do you feel about their presence)? What do you see in the surrounding environment? With each question, I would encourage people to let themselves be surprised by what came to them in response.

Next, I would invite people to let the journey continue and watch where it led, giving them ample time for the journey to unfold. After a bit, I would invite people to also look back and see what they could about where they had come from (again encouraging them to be surprised by what they saw). And I would ask people, too, to look into the future to see just what they could about what might lie ahead on the journey.

After completing the visualization, I would have people open their eyes, turn to paper and crayons that I had provided, and draw what they remembered from the journey. I would encourage people to allow the journey and their experience of it to continue to unfold as they drew, to let the act of drawing further deepen the experience. I would also often have participants break up into small groups and share their journeys—encouraging people in the groups to ask curiosity questions as people told their stories. I would conclude by asking people what they would need to bring to their journey if it was to proceed in the most meaningful manner.

Emotional/Moral Intelligence:

If you want to engage emotional intelligence, you can read a novel or go to a play. To help people get in touch more actively with emotional intelligence in the Intensive, I would often combine the accessing of memories with journaling and role playing. I might start by having people close their eyes and reflect back through their lives, looking to times when feelings had had particular importance. I'd ask questions to help get a variety of emotions. I might suggest that people reflect on memories that involved different kinds of relationships—one with a friend, another with someone who might seem a competitor, another with a lover or a parent. Or I might suggest the accessing of memories from different ages, or perhaps memories where particular kinds of emotions stood out—a time when they felt frightened, angry, guilty, hurt, or a particularly deep sense of appreciation or caring.

Then I would have people pick out five or six of these memories that reflected different kinds of emotions and journal about the emotional qualities, exploring as deeply as they could while seeking words that might best give each feeling or emotion expression. I might also draw on active role playing—have people stand up and briefly speak as one or more of these qualities. Others in the group would ask questions and give feedback about how they had experienced what they had heard.

Finally, I would have people use crayons and paper to draw a "map" of these various feeling/emotional qualities, using the process to further deepen their relationship with each. I would have people notice the colors that they found themselves using to represent various qualities. I would also have people observe relationships, both between feeling/emotional qualities and themselves and between the various qualities—which they felt closest to, which most distant, which seemed to clash, which seemed more associated. I'd have people notice if there were certain of these emotional constellations that they would need to learn more about if they wanted to grow. I'd also have people notice if there was one or more where the greatest challenge was to make boundaries to it, to be able to say "no" if it attempted to take over. I would encourage people to represent these various learnings on their feeling/emotion map.

Rational/Material Intelligence:

If you want to immerse yourself in the world of rationality, you can read some philosophy, do a math problem, or turn to a book on science. To engage the rational more actively and personally in the Intensive, I might first ask people how they saw themselves as thinking individuals. Did they think of themselves as pretty sharp, about average, someone for whom other capacities were stronger? And I might again have them draw on memories, this time reflecting on circumstances when they had been particularly called on to use their rational/analytic abilities.

I would then have participants reflect rationally on their experiences with each of the other intelligences, to note what insights they could glean from analyzing what had happened with each of the previous exercises. I would encourage people to see if they could find patterns, discern important lessons, tease apart strengths and weakness. And I would have people again turn to their journals, this time to make a summary analysis of their experience and what they had learned.

Finally, I would have people step back and reflect on the analyses they had just written. I'd ask them first what the act of bringing this more analytic lens to their experiences with each exercise added to understanding. I'd then ask them the complementary question, what might be missing in the analysis for which other ways of knowing they had drawn on previously provided deeper access.

Integrative Meta-Perspective:

After doing these various intelligence-specific exercises, I'd have people reflect for a bit on what it might mean to more consciously draw on all of these ways of knowing in their daily lives. I'd have people again walk around the room, this time observing how the act of engaging the whole of intelligence's multiplicity simultaneously altered their experience of themselves, their sense of connection with others in the room, and their felt sense of the physical space. Depending on the context, I might also have people in some way put where the exercises had taken them into action. I might have people engage in conversation with others while consciously holding the whole of intelligence. Or I might have people take some time to ponder questions that had perplexed them in their lives and to see whether this fuller holding of the whole of intelligences in any way altered their relationship to the questions, or even suggested new answers.

Parts Work and Intelligence's Creative Multiplicity

One method proves particularly powerful for supporting culturally mature leadership and understanding. It also provides important further insight with regard to how our relationship to intelligence's creative multiplicity changes with Cultural Maturity's cognitive reordering. I call it simply Parts Work.

Parts Work as an approach is unusual in drawing simultaneously on all of intelligence's aspects. And it is unique as far as I know in doing so in a way that directly supports Integrative Meta-perspective. If Parts Work is done well and we are ready for the stretch, the technique gives us almost no choice but to engage understanding more maturely and systemically. The previous intelligence exercises provide good preparation for doing Parts Work. I describe the approach in depth and provide numerous examples in my comprehensive work, *Creative Systems Theory*.

CHAIRS REPRESENTING PARTS

CHAIR REPRESENTING
WHOLE-SYSTEM
PERSPECTIVE

In doing Parts Work, a person begins by envisioning various aspects of themselves—or perhaps aspects of a question that concerns them—like characters in a play. Leading from his or her Whole-Person/Whole-System (Integrative Meta-perspective) chair, the person engages the various parts set in chairs around the room in conversation, moving back and forth between the Whole-Person/Whole-System chair and the various parts. My job is to facilitate these conversations. Parts Work can also be done with more than one person to address larger cultural issues.

Parts Work follows three cardinal rules. Together these rules address Integrative Meta-perspective and its implications in a way that is quite precise. Each rule informs a particular aspect of culturally mature understanding.

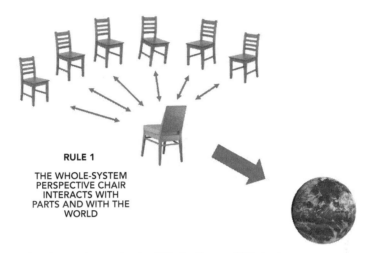

RULE 1

THE WHOLE-SYSTEM
PERSPECTIVE CHAIR
INTERACTS WITH
PARTS AND WITH THE
WORLD

The first rule: *Only the Whole-Person/Whole-System perspective chair interacts with parts and with the world.* It is the Whole-Person chair (or the Whole-System chair with larger cultural issues) that provides the leadership with Parts Work. This rule makes doing Parts Work an exercise for practicing culturally mature authority—in oneself and in the world.

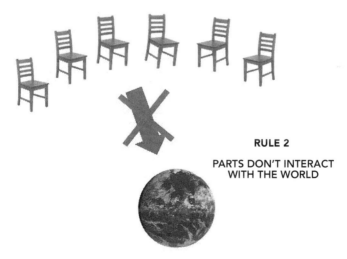

RULE 2

PARTS DON'T INTERACT
WITH THE WORLD

The second rule follows from the first: *Parts don't interact with the world.* A person doing Parts Work quickly recognizes that engaging the world from parts, while it is what most people do the larger portion of the time, produces limited and limiting results. People also come to recognize that ideological beliefs—whether political, religious, or those of competing belief systems within their particular professions—involve parts taking over and acting as if they have a relationship with the world.

RULE 3
PARTS DON'T INTERACT
WITH EACH OTHER

The third cardinal rule: *Parts don't interact with each other.* The recognition that parts don't talk to parts can take a bit longer to grasp, but it is ultimately just as critical. We can think of much in the internal struggles of daily life as cross-talk between competing parts. And the implications are just as significant collectively. Parts talking to parts is what has us easily confuse moderation or compromise with cultur-ally mature perspective, and ideological beliefs commonly have their roots in parts talking to parts. Creative Systems Theory describes how we can understand the back and forth between competing worldviews over the course of history as conversations between systemic parts.

The result when a person follows these cardinal rules is a kind of "cognitive rewiring." Wires are cut between both parts and the world, and between parts. And at the same time, people strengthen the wires that run between them-selves and the world, and also between themselves and their diverse and variously creative and contributing parts. Key to the power of the Parts Work approach is that the person doesn't need to be conscious of why it is working. Get the wiring right and culturally mature understanding and culturally mature leadership capacities are natural results.

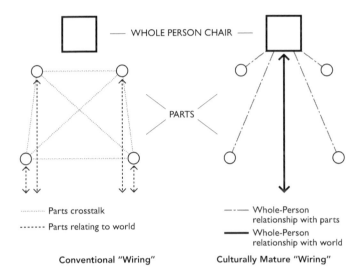

Fig. 4-1. Cultural Maturity's Cognitive Rewiring

As a therapist, I use Parts Work to help people address internal conflicts, explore relationships, and develop culturally mature leadership capacities. In think tank settings, I use it to address conflicting societal beliefs and to help people grasp how ideological conclusions that might seem incompatible may reflect aspects of a needed larger systemic picture.

Parts Work can also be used to engage overarching questions more systemically. In *Creative Systems Theory*, I offer an example that is particularly pertinent to appreciating how dramatically experience changes when we draw consciously on the whole of intelligence's creative multiplicity. I describe how the approach can help reconcile the most ultimate and timeless of polarities—that which divides the material and the spiritual, science and religion. Science draws preferentially on rational intelligence. Spirituality and religion through time have drawn preferentially on various of intelligence's nonrational aspects (body intelligence with spirituality's animistic beginnings, imaginal intelligence with polytheism's great pantheons of gods, and more emotional intelligence with monotheism's moral commandments). Parts Work, when done well, challenges the assumptions equally of someone who identifies with more scientific or more religious conclusions. The way it does highlights how culturally mature perspective's ability to hold the whole of intelligence is new in a fundamental sense. It also provides good illustration of the power of approaches like Parts Work that are able to draw on the whole of intelligence's creative multiplicity.

Someone of more scientific bent doing Parts Work is likely, at least initially, to assume that a part that thinks rationally and scientifically appropriately sits in the Whole-Person/Whole-System chair. This is not an unreasonable assumption given where the person has often most found significance. But it is not too long before the person sees that there are many concerns, and concerns of no small importance, particularly in one's personal life—such as purpose or love—where this part is limited in what it has to contribute. Eventually, the person comes to recognize how more than this part is needed not just for making good personal life choices, but for the most filled-out and creative kind of science.

Something very similar tends to happen for people who identify with more spiritual sensibilities. This may be an individual with quite traditional religious beliefs, a person with more humanistic "spiritual but not religious" tendencies, or someone of more New Age bent. Commonly the person will assume that spiritual truth appropriately sits in the Whole-Person/Whole-System chair. Again, for them, this is not an unreasonable conclusion. But if the person of more spiritual/religious inclination works long enough, they recognize in a similar way that having spiritual truth sit in the Whole-Person/Whole-System chair in our time leads to problems. An all-too-common result is poorly thought-out life choices and unsuccessful relationships. It turns out that in a well-lived life—a spiritual life in the best sense—the more manifest parts of existence are as important as the essences. Eventually, the person may realize that holding the spiritual more systemically in this way will be key not just to making good everyday choices, but to the most full and creative relationship to spiritual experience.

In doing Parts Work, the chairs that advocate for aspects of larger truths—whether personal truths or truths of a more social or even more philosophical/existential sort—each in important ways add to the Whole-Person/Whole-System perspective chair's reflections. But they function at most as consultants. When we miss this fact, ultimately unhelpful—indeed, dangerous—specifically ideological conclusions result. With Parts Work, people confront this recognition not just as some abstract conclusion, but personally and immediately. Living from the Whole-Person/Whole-System chair—and with it, drawing on the whole of our cognitive complexity—defines the task with culturally mature understanding and leadership, whether in our personal lives or more broadly. We can think of doing so as what ultimately defines today's needed new common sense. The fact that the Parts Work method draws on the whole of intelligence is key to how it provides this result.

CHAPTER FIVE

Creative Context and Intelligence's Multiplicity

One of the most striking recognitions when we step into Cultural Maturity's new territory of experience is how dramatically truth becomes contextual. When we leave behind history's shared parental absolutes and a time's more particular ideological beliefs, we are confronted by the fact that what matters depends on when and where we look. At first, such contextual relativity can be difficult to grasp. We are more used to thinking of significance as once-and-for-all and absolute. Or if we do acknowledge the role of context, we are likely to stop with postmodern, anything-goes assumptions. One of the most important consequences of Cultural Maturity's cognitive reordering is that it allows us to make highly precise discernments that are precise precisely because they take contextual nuance into account.

We can think of Creative Systems Theory's framework for understanding purpose, change, and interrelationship in human systems as a set of tools for making culturally mature context-specific distinctions. That it succeeds at doing so brings us back to the topic of this book. We can understand the theory's ability to address context in terms of how Integrative Meta-perspective provides a more direct connection with intelligence's multiple aspects. When we draw on the whole of intelligence's creative multiplicity and do so in the needed more conscious and integrative ways, the fact that truth is contextual becomes obvious.

Here I'll reflect briefly on two kinds of contextual relativity addressed by the theory, giving particular attention to intelligence's role in addressing them. We've caught a glimpse of the first—what the theory calls Patterning in Time—with Chapter Two's look at how intelligence's multiplicity manifests in specific ways with each stage in any creative/formative process. Patterning in Space notions address here-and-now contextual relativity. They make a similarly more dynamic and nuanced kind of discernment for systemic differences at specific points in time—for example, between domains in culture, academic disciplines, groups with different ideological leanings, or individuals with differing personality styles. The Creative Systems Personality Typology provides the most developed set of Patterning in Space distinctions in the theory.

Patterning in Time

Patterning in Time concepts highlight how culturally mature decision-making requires being keenly attentive to temporal context. With maturity in our personal development, we get a beginning sense of such relativity as it pertains to our individual lives. We better recognize how different experience can be depending on when in our lives it takes place. We may also come to better appreciate differences that are a function of where we are developmentally in activities we engage in— in a relationship, in a job, in a particular creative endeavor. Such temporal perspective is part of what we call wisdom.

With Cultural Maturity, we gain a similar ability to step back and recognize the role of change in how we understand more broadly. That includes an even deeper and more developed appreciation for such more personal-scale, change-related differences. And of particular importance, it also includes more encompassing, cultural-level temporal understanding. Sensitivity to one's temporal context at a cultural level has always been important, but in times past it came with being immersed in one's cultural time—like water to a fish. Integrative Meta-perspective is needed if we are to consciously and deeply understand ourselves in the context of cultural time. And certainly it is necessary if we are to appreciate the temporal contexts of others.

As far as that deeper appreciation for personal-scale change-related differences that comes with culturally mature understanding, applying developmental perspective to individual psychological growth is today generally accepted. But it is important to recognize that even that is quite recent. I've noted the influence of Jean Piaget's work early on in my thinking. His ideas were then groundbreaking. Concepts that apply evolutionary perspective to cultural change tend not only to be less recognized, in certain academic circles can they can be specifically suspect, if not outright dismissed. This is in part for good reasons. Evolutionary thinking has been used in times past to justify racism and colonialism. But the primary reason is likely deeper. It turns out that it takes Integrative Meta-perspective and its fuller engagement with intelligence's multiplicity to appreciate cultural evolution in any deep way.

Chapter Two's look at how intelligence manifests in different ways with each stage in creative/formative process introduced the connection. With Cultural Maturity's cognitive changes and the capacity to engage our multiple intelligences more directly and more fully, we become better able to recognize the particular kinds of richness that order the realities of different cultural times. The ability to make sense of cultural change in a way that is deeply affirming of human experience, whatever the period in culture, lets us get beyond past objections to evolutionary perspective. The result is a nuance and complexity of understanding that is essential if we are to effectively move forward.

My book *Creative Systems Theory* examines how Patterning in Time notions and their foundation in an appreciation for intelligence's creative multiplicity apply to developmental dynamics of all sorts—a simple creative act, personal psychological development, how love relationships change, how organizations change, and the evolution of culture. Below is a chart from the book that summarizes some of these striking parallels. In it I include the formal terms that the theory uses for the various creative stages— Pre-Axis for creation's "incubation stage," Early-Axis for "inspiration stage" dynamics, Middle-Axis for creation's "perspiration stage," and Late-Axis for its "finishing and polishing" stage. You will see the reason for including this more formal language shortly when we turn to Patterning in Space distinctions.

CREATIVE STAGES

MAJOR PERIODICITIES

	Pre-Axis	Early-Axis	Middle-Axis	Late-Axis	Transition	Integrative Stages
A CREATIVE EVENT	Incubation	Inspiration	Perspiration	Finishing & Polishing	Presentation	Becoming "Second Nature" (Integration of the newly created form into self and culture)
A LIFETIME	Prenatal Period & Infancy	Childhood	Adolescence	Early Adulthood	Midlife Transition	Mature Adulthood (From knowledge to wisdom—integration of self as formed identity with the ground of being)
A RELATIONSHIP	Pre-relationship	Falling in Love	Time of Struggle	Established Relationship	Time of Questioning	Mature Intimacy (Relationship as two whole people—marriage of the "loved" and the "lover" within each person)
THE HISTORY OF CULTURE	Pre-History	Golden Ages	Middle Ages	Age of Reason	Transitional Culture	Cultural Maturity (Larger meeting of the form and context of culture)

Fig. 5-1 Patterning in Time[1]

Patterning in Time and History

The way Integrative Meta-perspective alters our relationship to history provides one of the best ways to appreciate the power of applying intelligence's creative multiplicity to our understanding of change. Oscar Wilde wrote, "The one duty we owe to history is to rewrite it." By bringing culturally mature evolutionary perspective and intelligence's creative multiplicity to how we address history, Creative Systems Theory's application of a creative frame does just that.

Its contribution in this regard has multiple layers. Most immediately, drawing creatively on the whole of intelligence results in a more dynamic picture of history, one that in new ways comes alive. Traditional notions of history tend to reduce the past to a chronicling of leaders, wars, and technologies. And more recent "big history" efforts rarely get us much further. The picture provided by a creative frame at the least has as much to do with ourselves as what we might invent. And ultimately it has to do with something more fundamental—how collectively we create the structures of human societies and the truths on which we base our lives.

Creative Systems Theory Patterning in Time concepts also help us see history more accurately. Certainly this is the case where traditionally we have denigrated the realities of earlier cultural times. Patterning in Time observations provide an appreciation for what makes the realities of various chapters in humanity's story powerful and unique, including those we may before have painted darkly. It is here that they most directly address the legitimate concerns that have often in times past resulted in the dismissal of evolutionary thinking.

---

1 You will notice that the chart includes a depiction of how polarity evolves over the course of any creative/formative process. Previously, I've described how the distance between polar opposites increases with each stage in formative process's first half and how formative process's second half involves more specifically integrative dynamics. CST calls this progression the Creative Function.

Just as much, Patterning in Time concepts help us see history more accurately where in the past we have romantically idealized particular cultural realities. Such idealizations have taken different forms depending on the time in culture that was romanticized.[2] But whatever the particular reference, Integrative Meta-perspective similarly helps us leave behind this more elevating sort of projective distortion. Cultural Maturity's cognitive reordering provides a clearer, if not always so reflexively affirming, picture of the past.

Patterning in Time notions also contribute by making how we understand history deeper and more complete. Even when denigrating and idealizing have not distorted our perceptions, the sensibilities that have defined Modern Age thought have caused us to miss much that is most important. Culturally Mature perspective helps us better recognize how aspects of history to which we may have given secondary importance at best—such as art, music, religion, moral belief, or the life of the body—in fact have considerable pertinence to making sense of the past. And it turns out that what we have missed has often been exactly that which is most essential not to miss if we wish to make sense of values, motivations, and worldviews—particularly those of premodern peoples (including ourselves prior to the Industrial Age). With Cultural Maturity's cognitive reordering, these added ingredients stop being condiments and become explicit parts of the main meal.

---

2 Romantic idealization can make association with any cultural stage. Academics may idealize the Age of Reason (or sometimes the ancient Greeks). Adamant conservative and fundamentalist religious views can by inference idealize almost medieval sensibilities (drawing on belief from a time previous to modern secular humanism and after the rise of monotheism). And New Age ideologies, along with the beliefs of environmentalists and certain feminists, may draw on idealized references to cultural times and places where archetypally feminine sensibilities held clear influence—for example, to tribal cultures, early agrarian societies, and classical Eastern belief.

As important, Patterning in Time notions provide a picture that makes history as much about "why" as about "what." Culturally mature developmental/evolutionary perspective helps us better put past events in context and grasp how one moment of history ties to another—insights that can radically alter how we interpret circumstances. It transforms history from a chronicling of events and beliefs to a multifaceted study of human purpose and our relationship to it. While purpose has always been a part of well-told history, when we consciously bring more of ourselves to the task of understanding, history becomes more specifically an inquiry into who we are as storytellers and makers of meaning. Also, by implication, history becomes as much about the possible nature of meaning in the future as it is about the stories that have brought us to where we are today.

Finally, Creative Systems Theory Patterning in Time notions suggest an important "historical" reward beyond history itself. They make the study of history a hands-on tool for acquiring culturally mature perspective. Just as practicing needed new leadership capacities or more deeply engaging the complexities of intelligence can bring us closer to culturally mature understanding, so too can a sufficiently deep engagement with where we have come from. Grasping history more deeply can provide a particularly powerful way to realize the more complete kind of understanding that future tasks of all sorts will increasingly require of us.

Patterning in Space

Creative Systems Theory's approach to understanding contextual relativity is unusual in that it addresses both temporal distinctions and here-and-now differences. It is unique as far as I know in conceptually linking these two kinds of contextual relativity. In times past, if we've acknowledged contextual differences at all, we've assumed that these two kinds of differences were distinct concerns. I've noted how Creative Systems Theory uses the same creative language when making Patterning in Time and Patterning in Space distinctions.

With Integrative Meta-perspective—and specifically with the application of a creative frame—we find that a related kind of mapping helps us understand both change and interrelationship in human systems.

Creative Systems Theory describes how human systems pattern creatively not just over time, but also in the here and now. Biological systems inhabit ecological niches. Creative Systems Theory proposes that human systems similarly differentiate into a predictable array of creatively ordered psychological/ social niches. Patterning in Space concepts address diversity within human systems of all scales—domains in a society, departments in a university, professions, functions in a business, roles in a family, personality styles, or parts within ourselves. Over the years, Patterning in Space distinctions have provided many of Creative Systems Theory's most fascinating insights. They've also offered some of the most rewarding—and fun— interactions with colleagues and students.

While Creative Systems Patterning in Space concepts are pertinent any time our interest lies with human here-and-now systemic differences, it is with personality style differences that this aspect of the theory had its beginnings and also where it has been most developed. The Creative Systems Personality Typology (CSPT) presents a nuanced and detailed framework for teasing apart and articulating temperament differences.

It is remarkable how different people can be as a product of temperament. Just as remarkable is how blind we can be to this fact. If we take time to understand personality diversity at all deeply, it can be hard to imagine that teachers could teach effectively without such understanding or that psychologists could in any way be of help. And we find such blindness with the most learned of people. As with Patterning in Time's evolutionary notions, attempts within academia to delineate and articulate personality differences tend not to be widely acknowledged and are often simply dismissed.[3]

---

3 The one exception is the Myers-Briggs typology (based on the work of Carl Jung) that is often used by people in psychology and

It is reasonable to ask how it is that we have tended to miss this profundity of difference. I suspect the reason is related. Again we find a kind of distinction where understanding requires that we draw on the whole of intelligence's multiplicity. We need to get at least a toe in Cultural Maturity's new territory of experience if this kind of difference is to make deep sense.

The Creative Systems Personality Typology provides a way to understand not just the specific strengths and weaknesses of different personality styles, but also how various styles can best work together. It also offers a framework for understanding how personality diversity interplays with other kinds of human difference, such as gender and ethnic diversity. And it provides perspective for making sense of the experiences of people with different temperaments at specific points in developmental processes. It has particular significance for its power as a tool for supporting the kind of creative collaboration on which a healthy future will more and more depend.

A bare-boned look at how Creative Systems Theory approaches temperament differences begins with the recognition that people with different personality styles are most gifted with regard to the various sensibilities that I've associated with specific stages in formative process. (They most embody the intelligences and relationships between polar tendencies needed to support stage-specific creative tasks.) Using Creative Systems Theory language, more "Early-Axis" types have greatest natural affinity with more "inspiration stage" sensibilities, more "Middle-Axis" types with more "perspiration stage" sensibilities, and more "Late-Axis" types with more "finishing and polishing" sensibilities.

We can identify the basic contours of Early-, Middle-, and Late-Axis personality differences fairly readily in the goings-on of daily life. (As I will get back to, Pre-Axial personality dynamics represent a special case in modern culture.) For example,

---

business consulting. But the CSPT engages differences with significantly greater depth and with implications that more directly address the tasks of Cultural Maturity.

within a business, we have the wild creatives and nerdy "egg-heads" over in research and development. We also have the managers and workers who take R and D's innovations and get them first into a practical form and then into production. And we have the marketing and financial types who add ideas about what is needed to make the product attractive to its buyers, take care of money matters, and do the selling.

The fact of Early-, Middle-, and Late-Axis difference is only the starting point when applying the typology. Within each personality style axis, the theory also distinguishes more Upper and Lower, Outer and Inner "aspects" and personality constellations. We know these differences from everyday experience. Some people live most from their heads or from similarly elevated spiritual aspects of experience, while others are more down to earth. Some people give greatest attention to more in-the-world concerns, while with others more personal, internal elements in experience have the greater importance.

On the CSPT website (www.CSPThome.org) and in the book *Creative Systems Theory*, I go into detail with regard to each of the theory's basic temperament patterns. Here I will touch only on the basic contours of the typology, giving particular attention to the role of intelligence's multiplicity. In describing each personality style axis, I will note how it preferentially engages and applies specific aspects of our cognitive complexity. Later I will come back and fill out these basic intelligence-related observations as I did with Patterning in Time. In a similar way, with each personality style pattern, along with one intelligence having primary influence, we can find each of the other intelligences present, but in a secondary way specific to that temperament axis.

Pre-Axial Patterns:

Pre-Axial patterns differ from other temperament constellations in that they rarely manifest in modern times as primary dynamics in healthy individuals (the one exception being people with a strongly Pre-Axial cultural background). Because such dynamics are principally of interest to those in the helping professions, they are beyond the scope of this discussion of normal variation. I will observe simply that body intelligence tends to play a major role in how they process experience.

Early-Axis Patterns:

Early-Axis temperaments reflect a special affinity with the inspiration stage in formative process—that period when the buds of new creation first find their way into the world of the manifest. The Early's defining intelligence is the imaginal, the language of symbol, myth, and metaphor (for the modern Early, as experienced within the rational/ material context of today's Late-Axis culture), with body intelligence playing a secondary role. The reality of the Early-Axis individual is born from the organizing sensibilities that give us possibility and innovation.

A few notable Earlies from history: Leonardo da Vinci, Georgia O'Keeffe, Rainer Maria Rilke, Isadora Duncan, Mary Cassatt, Howard Hughes, John Coltrane, Boris Karloff, Pablo Picasso, Frank Zappa, Nikola Tesla, Jack Nicholson, and Mrs. Saunders (my kindergarten teacher). More notorious Earlies include Charles Manson, David Kaczynski, and Rasputin.

The pivotal role of imaginal intelligence is most explicit with Early/Uppers. I am reminded of Albert Einstein's famous assertion, "I am interested in God's thoughts; the rest are details." Or from Lewis Carroll in *Through the Looking Glass*: "'Contrariwise,' continued Tweedledee, 'if it was so, it might be; and if it were so, it would be: but as it isn't, it ain't. That is logic.'" With Early/Lowers, body intelligence can play at least as great a role. Early/Lowers tend to be more comfortable in their bodies than other temperaments and derive particular fulfillment through bodily experience. Indeed, for Early/Lowers body and spirit can be hard to distinguish. Salvador Dali once exclaimed, "I don't do drugs—I am drugs."

Where do we find Earlies? Often they work with young children (a grade school teacher, a day-care worker). Frequently they become artists—visual artists (particularly those of more abstract inclination), dancers (particularly those whose aesthetic tends toward the improvisational), musicians (most jazz musicians, some classical and many rock and roll musicians), or writers (particularly poets and most writers of science fiction). Earlies also make important contributions in the sciences. (Many of science's major innovators have been Earlies—though the larger number of scientists are Lates.) Recently, Earlies have starred in the high-tech revolution. (Steve Jobs, Bill Gates, and Elon Musk are all Earlies.) Most people who teach reflective techniques such as meditation and yoga are Earlies. (It is Earlies who are most attracted to things spiritual, particularly practices with roots in Early-Axis cultural times.)

Middle-Axis Patterns:

Middle-Axis temperaments most strongly embody the "perspiration" stage sensibilities that we find as new creation struggles into crude, but now solid, manifestation. While Earlies identify most with the first improvisational sparks of creation, Middles find greatest meaning turning sparks into usable fire. Emotional-moral intelligence, the intelligence of heart and guts (as it manifests within Late-Axis culture) orders the Middle's world.

A few notable Middles from history: Teddy Roosevelt, Mother Teresa, Margaret Thatcher, Joe Louis, Billy Graham, Babe Ruth, Florence Nightingale, Colin Powell, Aretha Franklin, Julia Child, Queen Victoria, Johnny Cash, J. Edgar Hoover, Cesar Chavez, and Betty Friedan. More notorious Middles include Joseph Stalin, Adolf Hitler, Ma Barker, and Jesse James.

The harder aspects of emotional-moral intelligence—the stuff of guts and fortitude—dominate with Middle/Upper and Middle/Outer temperaments. From Winston Churchill, "This is a lesson: Never give in—never, never, never, never." From Samuel Johnson, "Great works are performed not by strength, but by perseverance."

The stuff of the heart holds sway in Middle/Inner and Middle/Lower temperaments, where the archetypally feminine is strongest. From Margaret Mead, "One of the oldest human needs is having someone wonder where you are when you don't come home at night." From Abraham Lincoln, "The better part of a man's life consists of his friendships."

Middles often become teachers, managers in business, social workers, soldiers, athletes and coaches, union bosses, ministers or priests, physicians (about an equal balance of Middle/Upper and Late/Upper), politicians (a similar balance), police officers, fire fighters, bankers, loggers, owners of family businesses, machinists, miners, or carpenters. In addition, Middles make up the greater portion of stay-at-home parents. (It is with Middle-Axis that we find the strongest identification with home, family, and community.) Women who think of themselves first as wives and mothers are commonly Middles, as are the most devoted husbands and fathers. Middle-Axis individuals frequently play strong roles in their neighborhoods and churches, and in social service organizations. Most of the "real work" in society is done by Middles.

Late-Axis Patterns:

Late-Axis patterns correspond to the finishing and polishing stage in formative process. People with Late-Axis temperaments draw on sensibilities that make them particularly gifted when it comes to tasks of detail and completion. Here rational/material intelligence orders experience, bringing emphasis to the intellect and to the more refined (manifest) aspects of the emotional and the aesthetic.

Some notable Lates from history: Walter Cronkite, Marie Curie, Carl Sagan, Julia Roberts, Sammy Davis, Jr., Elizabeth Taylor, Frank Sinatra, Gloria Steinem, Woodrow Wilson, Johnny Carson, Clark Gable, Mikhail Baryshnikov, William F. Buckley, and Robert Redford. Less savory sorts tend to engage in white collar crime, so are less visible and less often prosecuted than Early and Late lawbreakers—Michael Milkin comes to mind, along with those involved in the investment bank excesses of the 2008 financial collapse.

The aspects of rational/material intelligence that most stand out with people of Late/Upper temperament are clarity of thought, verbal facility, and the ability to deal easily and effectively with the material world. From John F. Kennedy, "In times of turbulence and change, it is more true than ever that knowledge is power." From Elizabeth Cady Stanton, "In a word, I am always busy, which is perhaps the chief reason I am always well." With Late/Lower personalities, the aesthetic combines with more material aspects of emotional intelligence. From Alfred, Lord Tennyson, "'Tis better to have loved and lost, than never to have loved at all." Estee Lauder offered this advice: "Never just 'run out for a few minutes' without looking your best. This is not vanity—it is self-liking."

Lates often become professors, writers, lawyers, CEOs, scientists, fashion models, ballet or modern dancers, Wall Street financiers, marketers, or actors. More frequently than with people from other axes, various individuals can differ widely in their inclinations.[4] Within Late-Axis we find the people who are most rational in their perspective, and also those who tend most toward the romantic. We find the people who are most materialistically driven, and at once many of those most committed to artistic and intellectual pursuits where monetary remuneration can be slight. We find the people most aggressively in the world, and also many of those most internal and reflective in their proclivities.

With Late/Upper/Inners, the more intellectual of these qualities stand out. University professors, scientific researchers, and nonfiction writers commonly have Late/Upper/Inner personalities. With Late/Upper/Outers, more

---

4 A look to the Creative Function provides explanation. It is here that we see the greatest natural separation between poles.

external and material concerns take center stage. Here we commonly find the people who are most facile with money and the complexities of the business world—corporate executives, economists, media moguls, and stockbrokers. With Late/Lower patterns, qualities such as social ease, talent, sensuality, and emotional presence often most stand out. Of all personality groups, Late/Lowers are most likely to enjoy being "on stage." People in the performing arts tend to have at least some Late/Lower in their makeup, as do the great majority of fashion models and television entertainers. Late/Lower/Inner is a common personality style of dancers and actors. With Late/Lower/Outers we find the people with the greatest capacity to project and be visible. They define the entertainment industry. Glamour and celebrity are Late/Lower/Outer words.

More than one temperament, one intelligence:

I've noted an important Patterning in Space intelligence-related recognition that we also encounter with Patterning in Time. While one intelligence has primary influence with each personality style pattern, we also find each of the other intelligences present in a secondary way specific to that temperament axis. Appreciating how this is so helps fill out our understanding of each temperament constellation. It also further deepens our understanding of each of intelligence's multiple aspects by highlighting the diverse ways in which it can manifest. And there is a further implication. The fact that we find such nuance in parallels between Patterning in Time and Patterning in Space distinction provides further confirmation of the power of a creative frame and the kind of cognitive reordering that Creative Systems Theory describes with the concept of Integrative Meta-perspective.

Below I've drawn on language from the chart in Chapter Three (Figure 3-1) with a few reflections that help tie observations to temperament distinctions. The important recognition is that with very little adjustment, the same words apply equally well to making temporal and here-and-now contextual observations. (Again I should note that finding good words for these more detailed distinctions necessarily presents a challenge, particularly where intelligences don't function at the level of language.)

Body Intelligence: I've observed that body intelligence is primary with Pre-Axis. The way I describe it in the chart— "the creature body/the body as nature"—works pretty well. In the chart, I describe the Early-Axis body as "the body as essence/the body of ritual/the spirit or dream body." A term like "energetic body" works better when thinking about personality dynamics. It is how we experience the body when doing yoga or meditating. The way the chart describes the Middle-Axis body—"the visceral-muscular body/the body of heart and guts"—again works adequately. It is the bodily reality that we most associate with being an athlete and that we feel most directly in relationships. In the chart, I describe the Late-Axis body as "the physical body/the body as appearance." This is the body as experienced when we say we "have" a body (as if it was separate from us). It is also the body that Sophia Loren was referring to when she observed that "sex appeal is fifty percent what you've got and fifty percent what people think you've got."

Imaginal Intelligence: While the symbolic has its strongest influence with Early-Axis temperaments, it similarly plays a role and takes particular manifestations with each axis. In the chart, I describe its role with Pre-Axis as "animism—the symbolic as a language of nature." This fits as well for temperament as it does for creative stage. For Early-Axis, the chart describes imaginal intelligence's manifestation as "myth—the symbolic as a language of ritual and inspirational relationship." With Early-Axis temperaments, it works better to think of it in terms of creative imagination. The chart describes Middle-Axis imaginal expression as "legend—the symbolic as a language of moral order." With Middle-Axis personality styles, we might think of the symbolism a person associates with their particular religious or national affiliations. In the chart, I describe imaginal intelligence as it manifests in Late-Axis as "fantasy—the symbolic as a language of romanticism and idealism." The word "fantasy" works pretty well for temperament as well as development. Here we find the more surface kind of imagination found on a visit to Disneyland.

Emotional Intelligence: I've observed that emotional intelligence's influence is primary with Middle-Axis temperaments. Its role is less explicit with Pre-Axis, but the chart's description of "feeling as harmony with nature" certainly implies emotional sensibility. The kind of body intelligence that is primary at this stage can be deeply felt. The chart describes emotional intelligence in Early-Axis with the words "feeling as inspiration, essence, and primal passion." That works pretty well for emotional intelligence's manifestation with Early-Axis temperament. How the chart describes emotional intelligence with Middle-Axis—"feeling as visceral emotion"—works adequately all the way around. I've described emotional intelligence as the intelligence of "heart and guts." That kind of language is most in keeping with its Middle-Axis manifestations. The chart describes the feeling dimension with Late-Axis as "feeling as sentiment and pleasure." That continues to work well for temperament, particularly as it manifests with Late/Lower patterns.

Rational Intelligence: While the intellect takes most developed manifestation with Late-Axis in both time and space, every temperament axis has its own version of verbal/ideational expression rooted in its underlying sensibilities. In the chart, I refer to its presence with Pre-Axis as "participatory consciousness." While body intelligence is primary with Pre-Axial dynamics, there is at least self-concept and with it ideas about the connectedness of experience. With Early-Axis in the chart, I refer to "magical and aesthetic thought". Early/Uppers in particular often think in highly sophisticated ways, but their ideas ultimately serve creative insight. With Middle-Axis, the chart refers to "the logic of right and wrong." That works pretty well for Patterning in Space as well as Patterning in Time. The ideas of Middles tend to make reference in some way to issues of morality, competence, relationship, or control. The chart speaks of rational intelligence with Late-Axis as "Rational, material thought." With regard to temperament, here we find rational logic of the academic sort. We also find particular acumen when it comes to finance. And particularly with Late/Lower, we find the kind of aesthetic distinctions that allow one to be adept at performance.

Temperament and the Tasks of Cultural Maturity

Any approach to understanding human differences can assist us in understanding ourselves and learning to better get along with others. But the Creative Systems Personality Typology, with how it directly engages the whole of intelligence's multiplicity, does so with a depth not found with other approaches. Of particular importance, while the typology describes the specifics of differences with particular detail, in addition it addresses mechanisms, helps us understand just why it is that we see the differences that we do. In the process, it also helps us better appreciate how such differences may contribute both to understanding what ultimately makes something true and to addressing what Cultural Maturity's changes ask of us.

One way the CSPT has direct pertinence to the tasks of Cultural Maturity concerns the importance of separating the wheat from the chaff in our thinking. It turns out that we can predict the kind of ideological traps a person will be most vulnerable to by teasing apart psychological structures and patterns. This is the case both with regard to the kinds of social/political ideologies a person is most likely to ascribe to and common broader kinds of ideological affiliations (religious/philosophical/scientific). The typology describes how we can make a solid guess if we have information about temperament axis and aspects, and also about one further variable, what the theory calls Capacitance. (Capacitance refers to how much life a system can tolerate—think of a balloon, that if stretched too far, might break.)

Reflections from my years leading yearlong trainings at the Institute provide concrete illustration of where the CSPT's contribution to Cultural Maturity may be most ultimately significant. I would select participants for programs according to a couple of criteria. Capacitance is one—people needed to be "up to the task." But just as important, ultimately, was personality style. I chose participants so that temperament diversity was fully represented. One of the things that most struck people on the first day of the yearlong training was how different many of the people in the room were from the individuals that they were most used to spending time with. Because of the universally high Capacitance, these differences could not easily be dismissed.

Most immediately, having that diversity—and that particular kind of diversity—in the room was powerful at a personal level. One may never be a jazz musician, a professional football player, or an advertising executive, but if one can begin to understand what might make such people who they are—and better, even slightly embody their felt realities—these people's presence can help one more deeply engage creation's full systemic complexity in oneself. Partway through the year, I would engage the group in a deep immersion into the Creative Systems Personality Typology to help make these learnings more conscious.

Having that particular kind of diversity in the room also became essential for our shared work together. The mosaic of realities that personality style differences represent supported the collaborative efforts needed to address the deeply systemic questions these emerging culturally mature leaders were there to engage. Near the end of the training, I would have participants divide up into small think tank teams to work on the future of specific domains—education, government, business, and so on. By that time they had come to recognize that choosing like-minded team members was not the right approach if they wanted culturally mature results. If participants' teams were going to be most powerfully creative, they would need the contributions of each basic temperament axis.

Again, none of this would have been possible without Integrative Meta-perspective and the ability to draw actively on the whole of intelligence's creative multiplicity. Participants had developed the ability to engage intelligence's multiple aspects in part through the exercises that we did at the beginning of the year-long training. But they had also expanded this essential capacity through learning about and applying Creative Systems Theory's various context-discerning patterning concepts.

CHAPTER SIX

Further Reflections from the Vantage of Integrative Meta-Perspective and Intelligence's Creative Multiplicity

I'll conclude with a handful of brief pieces that highlight ways in which a more conscious and integrated relationship to intelligence's multiplicity alters experience. Each piece turns to a topic that I've addressed with greater detail in other books. Here I will give particular attention to the role that intelligence's creative multiplicity plays in providing needed insight.

We will start with a closer look at what I have spoken of as the Dilemma of Trajectory and examine some of the often quite crazy intelligence-related phenomena that it can produce. I will then turn to how the misuse of artificial intelligence could be the end of us and how the key to avoiding this fate lies with understanding the fundamental differences between machine intelligence and human intelligence. We will then examine how Cultural Maturity's cognitive reordering alters not just our relationship to intelligence, but also our understanding of conscious awareness, and with it, what it means to be a person. We will take a more detailed look at how Integrative Meta-perspective's "bridging"[1] of mind and body results in a very different picture of what it means to have a body. And finally, I will

---

1 I always put the word "bridging" in quotes to underline the distinction between the systemic reality that results from "bridging" and simple joining or oneness.

address how one of the places where nonrational aspects of intelligence take most direct manifestation—artistic expression—helps us appreciate the consequences of failing to address the Dilemma of Trajectory and what more will be required going forward.

The Dilemma of Trajectory, Transitional Absurdity, and the Exploitation of Intelligence's Multiplicity

I've suggested that while we tend to think of where history's progression has taken us as an ideal and end point, if it is, it could well mark the end of us. Those are strong sentiments. But hopefully I've at least begun to give a feel for how going no further would have unfortunate consequences, and also how a more mature and complete engagement with intelligence's deep complexities invites an important further kind of advancement.

I've briefly introduced how what Creative Systems Theory calls the Dilemma of Trajectory shines light on the easily precarious-seeming circumstance we find with our time. Expanding on how I have described intelligence through history provides additional insight. Along with offering entry into new ways of understanding, each chapter in culture's story has also distanced us from aspects of intelligence we have moved beyond. This distancing has served us. It has kept us from falling back into the more comfortable realities of times past. But something more is needed if we are to proceed. The Dilemma of Trajectory describes how continuing onward as we have threatens to distance us irretrievably from much that is most important in making us who we are. The topic is sufficiently important that it warrants further attention.

Framing the Dilemma of Trajectory in terms of the evolution of difference helps make its implications more concrete. Each stage in any developmental process's first half produces greater emphasis on difference—distance between polar extremes and difference more generally. At Transition, this defining impetus reaches an extreme. The Dilemma of

Trajectory brings attention to how going further in this direction really stops being an option. It is a dynamic that we witness at a personal scale with individual psychological development. Growth in the first half of life is marked by processes that produce ever-greater independence, individuality, and authority over the world around us—each expressions of increasing separation and emphasis on difference. But in an individual life's second half, this direction of change stops benefitting us in the same way. Indeed, if we continue on as we have, the second half of life becomes increasingly absurd, at best a thin caricature of youth.

The topic of leadership, what Cultural Maturity is ultimately about, provides a good way to frame the Dilemma of Trajectory at a cultural scale. Today, we confront profound questions—indeed, questions with god-like implications. But the authority needed to address them is not some ascension to a chair of final dominion (ourselves somehow becoming gods). It is also different from some further iteration of the Enlightenment's grand goal of bringing all of understanding into the pure light of awareness and realizing final control over the untamed. Indeed, many of the problems we face in today's world derive from just such hubristic notions of what right action is about. We are left in a pickle that cannot be resolved by continuing on the course we have known. If a more complete kind of understanding is in fact what today's new questions require, then culturally mature perspective—or at least something that provides a similar more aware and integrative outcome—becomes the only real option.

I've noted that Creative Systems Theory has a specific term—Transitional Absurdity—for what we find when we fail to appreciate the Dilemma of Trajectory and what it asks of us. When Modern Age sensibilities and assumptions are taken beyond their timeliness, they can become not just unhelpful, but, in effect, ludicrous. For a long time, I rarely used the notion publicly because of how easily it can contribute to cynicism. But as current circumstances on the planet more and more often reflect Transitional dynamics, the concept comes to have particular importance. When effectively understood, it provides essential insight for making sense of and addressing much that we see in today's world.

Transitional Absurdities take multiple forms. Some protect us simply by helping us ignore what is being asked of us. Denial in the face of critical environmental challenges such as climate change provides the most obvious example. Others more specifically "overshoot the mark," apply outmoded, onward-and-upward ways of thinking to questions that now demand much more of us. Techno-utopian beliefs at the least ignore that the ability to invent and the capacity to use invention wisely are not at all the same. We also encounter Transitional Absurdities that are better thought of as regressive reactions to feeling overwhelmed by the magnitude of current challenges. While some of today's extreme polarization in the social and political spheres may represent little more than the two-steps-forward-one-step-back nature of change or reactive responses to particular events, I suspect a major part of it reflects this specifically regressive sort of Transitional Absurdity.

For this book's focus, a couple of insights have particular pertinence. First is simply that Cultural Maturity's cognitive reordering, besides reconciling the Dilemma of Trajectory, also provides the needed antidote to Transitional Absurdity. Cultural Maturity's cognitive changes don't diminish challenges or eliminate overwhelm—indeed, they specifically contribute to our time's demands. But they do provide the more systemic kind of understanding needed to deal with current circumstances and what may lie ahead in the most healthy and effective ways.

The second kind of insight pertains more specifically to intelligence. Many of today's most consequential Transitional Absurdities involve the exploitation of intelligences that we have become distanced from with Transitional dynamics. Because we don't have ready access to these aspects of knowing in our time, we can be blind to when they are being used in exploitative ways. And because of their particular importance with Transition, at once we can easily be attracted to them and deeply affected by their presence even when they are being misused.

Many of today's most ultimately damaging Transitional Absurdities in some way involve the selling of pseudo-significance. They co-opt our attention for profit. We are particularly vulnerable to such co-opting when efforts engage the nonrational aspects of intelligence. Body intelligence, imaginal intelligence, and emotional intelligence each commonly suffer this kind of exploitative manipulation.

Violent content in the media provides a good example of the exploitative use of body intelligence, though the source of the greatest harm is different than one might think. Certainly such content normalizes violence. But more specifically with regard to body intelligence, today's constant barrage of violent imagery produces artificial stimulation that we easily confuse with meaning. Thirty years ago, I wrote an article expressing concern after seeing a movie where it was clear that the jolts of artificial stimulation that the movie's violent content provided were the main reason for the movie's existence. This kind of artificial stimulation in the name of meaning has today become increasingly pervasive, and not just with movies and television. Such mechanisms lie at the heart of the attraction of most video games.

We find imaginal intelligence similarly exploited in our time. The piece that concludes this chapter addresses how the fact that advertising has become today's preeminent art form has turned art's historical function on its head. For now, it is enough to note that advertising frequently draws us in by making use of the child-reality language of imaginal intelligence—for example, a talking toy car or a cute lizard or lion telling us what product to buy. And the addictive hold that digital "entertainment" can have on people often has its source in graphic novel–like mythic imagery applied in particularly dramatic ways.

The fact that we find emotional intelligence exploited is hardly new to current circumstances. Television soap operas and celebrity magazines in grocery store checkout lines have been familiar sources of emotional pseudo-fulfillment for years. But with emotional intelligence, too, we see it more and more often used in ways that exploit attention and lie to us about what is really important. Certainly we see this with "reality television" and the like. And if you want to find depictions of emotional intelligence at its most gratifying in the media, the best place to look again is advertising, with its promises of popularity and loving relationships if only we purchase this or that product. Where social media damages more than it informs, the mechanism of that harm most always comes back to how it exploits our tenuous relationship with emotional intelligence.

Today we are so used to such exploitative uses of body, imaginal, and emotional sensibilities that we rarely recognize that we are being manipulated. And certainly we don't recognize the depth of the damage that can result. But this changes when we appreciate the essential role that learning to draw in more conscious and mature ways on the whole of intelligence plays in culturally mature understanding. The importance of being of aware of such exploitation then becomes glaringly obvious.

Artificial Intelligence Versus the Real Thing

Appreciating intelligence's creative multiplicity derives a new kind of importance with the task of effectively managing the combined gifts and curses of the digital revolution. That importance comes into high relief with the task of addressing the risks and benefits of what people commonly refer to as "artificial intelligence." I prefer to call it machine intelligence or machine learning.

Machine intelligence should provide great benefits in times to come. But a growing number of prominent figures have warned of potentially dire consequences. I think the risks are very real. Unless we can learn to think about the potential dangers in more sophisticated ways, some of the most intriguing innovations of our time may very well prove to be our undoing. The essential insights for this book's reflections concern the fundamental differences between machine intelligence and human intelligence. It is those differences—and their major implications—that have me avoid the term "artificial intelligence."

Three mechanisms through which machine learning could have cataclysmic consequences are most often cited. In the first scenario, some kind of bad actor on the world stage wages a machine learning–based attack on a perceived enemy. The goal could be the destruction of physical infrastructure such as electrical grids and water supplies, disruption of communications networks, or as we have seen attempted in very rudimentary form with Russian interference in elections, a fundamental undermining of social and governmental structures.

The second scenario is less obvious in its destructiveness, but it is where currently we see the greatest harm. Increasingly, today, our electronic devices are designed to capture our attention, pretty much whatever it takes to do so. And machine learning plays an increasing role in how they accomplish this. As a psychiatrist, I consider device addiction one of today's most pressing concerns. The mechanisms with device addiction are essentially the same as those that produce the attraction of addicting drugs. Our devices create artificial stimulation that substitutes for the bodily feedback that would normally tell us that something matters. Today, machine learning algorithms compound those mechanisms many times over, supporting the creation of ever more powerful digital designer drugs—with increasingly destructive results.

The third kind of scenario is what people in the tech world most often point toward when they warn that AI could be the end of us. Systems applying machine learning could very well come to out-compete us. It is easy to make the goal of a machine learning algorithm simply to have the mechanism propagate itself. Such algorithms can be single-minded in their competitiveness in ways that we humans will never be, and would never want to be. (In spite of often thinking of ourselves as competitive in a simplistic Darwinian fight-for-survival sense, we—thankfully—are more complex than just this.) The fact that learning with such systems can take place autonomously and is often beyond our ability to decipher, much less control, means that we face the real risk of runaway mechanisms where the destruction of humanity, if not an outright intent, becomes an unintended consequence.

These last two scenarios taken together create what may well be our time's greatest existential danger—a greater threat to our well-being than nuclear weaponry, climate change, or global disease. The most likely way that machine learning will out-compete us is through the creation of ever more effective addiction and distraction. It may not be through being smarter than we are, but by making us stupid—and trivial. This would require no ill intent. Give a machine learning algorithm the simple instruction to increase traffic to a website, for example, and with time, the most addictive of possible strategies will be the result. Addictive distraction is the most reliable way to maximize eyeballs. Machine learning's role in producing a world in which distraction and addiction more and more often replace meaningful human activity could very well be the way it ultimately contributes most directly to our undoing.

These possibilities are legitimately scary. And in their beginning manifestations, they are realities we already live with. It could easily seem that there is nothing we can do. If the machines want to take over, eventually they will. This is the conclusion that many people in the tech world aware enough to be concerned seem to be reaching.

But while this may well be our fate, I don't think it needs to be. The missing piece is the simple recognition that machine learning and human intelligence have very different mechanisms. In fact, they have very little in common. Machine learning mimics but one part of intelligence—our rationality—and that only in limited ways. (Our rationality in fact functions in ways that are much more nuanced than we tend to assume.)

An essential observation that follows from those differences is critical to how human intelligence can serve as a buffer to potential dangers.

I've made reference to it in speaking of how Integrative Meta-perspective provides an antidote to today's Crisis of Purpose. While machine learning is single-minded in pursuing its goal, human intelligence is inherently more complex—and creative—in its workings. When I engage with someone around questions of purpose in therapy, I rarely think in terms of specific goals. I know that if I can help the person more deeply connect with the whole of themselves, a greater sense of purpose and more purposeful life choices will be the result. There is an important sense in which human intelligence is by its nature purpose-centered.

With regard to more collective questions, there is an important related sense in which human intelligence is not just more complex and purposeful in its considerations, it is by its nature moral.

That may seem a rather questionable claim given how frequently we are not at all moral in our everyday dealings. And given how often history reveals acts of which we should not at all be proud, it might seem preposterous. But most often in our daily lives we act with basic kindness. And when we look at history's big picture, we find humanity bringing ever greater complexity to its moral discernments.

The important point is that there is clearly something in what it means to be human that is allied not just with advantage, but with purpose and larger good. And it is embedded deeply enough that we can think of the human narrative as a whole as a story of evolving purpose and moral capacity. Human intelligence by its nature engages us in questions of value and meaning. When it comes to addressing the dangers that potentially accompany machine learning, this distinction is critical. Machine learning is a tool, and one with great potential for good. But in contrast with human intelligence, there is nothing in it that makes it inherently good. Put bluntly, machine intelligence is not really intelligence.

Today, we easily miss this critical difference. Indeed, because we so readily idealize the technological (in effect make it our god), we can get things turned around completely. Caught in techno-utopian bliss, we can make machine learning what we celebrate. We do so at our peril. Our ultimate task as toolmakers is to be sure that we use our ever more amazing tools not just intelligently, but wisely. That starts with being able to clearly distinguish ourselves and our tools. Machine learning will provide a particularly defining test of this essential ability, one on which our very survival may depend. Passing that test will require the deeper engagement with intelligence's creative multiplicity that comes with Cultural Maturity's cognitive reordering.

Conscious Awareness and
Intelligence's Creative Multiplicity

Integrative Meta-perspective, as I've described it, involves at once a stepping back that expands awareness and a new and deeper engagement with the full complexity of cognition's workings. Thus far, I've given primary attention to that deeper engagement, and in particular to its role in connecting us with intelligence's multiple aspects. But changes in how we understand awareness are as striking and similarly important. They will be critical not just to making effective choices, but also to any at all complete future understanding of identity.

The topic of awareness in fact is where most people start when they first encounter the concept of Culture Maturity. They rightly think of greater awareness as Cultural

Maturity's defining achievement. But this observation is of limited use—indeed, it can easily lead us astray—if we don't appreciate how conscious awareness, too, is changing. Cultural Maturity's cognitive reorganization doesn't just increase awareness, it also alters how we understand the nature and functioning of awareness. It gives awareness a new, at once more humble and more powerful, expressly creative role. Integrative Meta-perspective's new, more complete picture of who we are and how we understand can make full sense only with an appreciation for this new kind of significance.

The recognition that awareness is important to consider is nothing new. Pulitzer-prize–winning author John Noble Wilford beautifully summed it up: "Alone among all creatures, the species that styles itself wise, *Homo sapiens*, has an abiding interest in its distant origins, knows that its allotted time is short, worries about the future and wonders about the past." And awareness' contribution has also always provoked debate—appropriately. Making sense of conscious awareness presents what might seem an unresolvable predicament. Using our conscious awarenesses to make sense of conscious awareness is a bit like trying to touch one's nose with one's nose. I like Ambrose Bierce's definition in his *Devil's Dictionary*. "Mind: A mysterious form of matter secreted by the brain. Its chief activity consists in the endeavor to ascertain its own nature, the futility of the attempt being due to the fact that it has nothing but itself to know itself with." Arguably, awareness and what it makes possible, is what philosophy is most ultimately about.

But awareness's significance is today becoming different in ways that have major implications in every part of our lives. To understand these changes, it helps to recognize that awareness's role has changed before. We tend not to think of awareness as something that changes, at least in any sense other than how learning can help us to be "more aware." But awareness's mechanisms do change, and they are just as specific to particular times in development (within formative processes of all sorts) as everything else we have looked at.

Some of the most celebrated of historical change-points are awareness-related. We cannot be in the presence of ancient cave paintings without pondering the emergence of reflective awareness, and wondering just how and when that emergence took place. And if a single change most defined the Renaissance and the ensuing Enlightenment, it was awareness's new, more "objective," from-a-balcony role. In a whole new sense, we came to regard awareness as triumphant.

With Enlightenment objectivity, awareness became not just elevated, but also mythologized. The Enlightenment's grand task was to bring all of understanding into the light of awareness. Enlightenment thought made a new polarity ultimate truth: awareness, seen as linked with the rational, set in opposition to the subjective, a catch-all category to which all other intelligences along with simple errors in understanding were relegated. Conscious awareness became captain of the cellular ship. We came to equate it not just with truth, but with identity.

The changes that come with Cultural Maturity's new picture of awareness are just as significant as any of those previous. At least in the sense that Cultural Maturity provides perspective that helps us map the larger picture of how we have understood awareness at previous times in culture's story, it is arguably more so. But awareness's new significance is also central to the new kind of conceptual orientation that comes with Integrative Meta-perspective. I've described how awareness comes to stand separate from intelligence as a whole—including rationality. In this sense it becomes even more "objective." And, at the same time, awareness becomes more deeply engaged with intelligence's full creative complexity. Subjective and objective are "bridged." One result is a newly complete—differentiated and integrated—picture of intelligence.

Another is that our experience of awareness itself also changes—and radically. Its function becomes creative in a new, more explicit sense.

The last century has provided significant glimpses into this new more creative picture. Many of the most important have come from my field of psychiatry and psychology. Few truths become more obvious when practicing the craft of the psychotherapist than how different the reality of conscious awareness is from the exalted way that the conscious mind has tended to view itself. Linking awareness and will back in the middle of the last century, psychiatrist Carl Jung put it this way in his book *Man and His Symbols:* "Where there's a will there's a way is the superstition of modern man." He went on to observe that "what we commonly call 'self-knowledge' is a very limited knowledge."

Actually, the fact that conscious awareness is limited in what it can grasp is exactly as things should be. The larger part of our functioning works best without volition's interference. (Recall the story of the centipede who walks gracefully with her hundred legs until praised for her exquisite memory.) The oft-used psychological metaphor that compares the psyche to an iceberg, part visible, part submerged, gets us started in the right direction (though unless applied carefully, it remains polar and polarizing[2]).

Awareness's new task is not to decide and control, but rather to be a creative catalyst and facilitator. It is to help us recognize as much of life's multihued complexity as we are able and to assist us in making the most life-affirming choices from the options revealed. This more explicitly creative role is more humble in the sense that it must give up its claim to final clarity. But at the same time it is more powerful in its ability to support both creative potency and that potency being applied in the most ultimately life-affirming ways. In a sense, awareness's function has always been creative—to

---

2 Recognizing the role that multiple intelligences necessarily play in cognition results in a more multilayered picture.

support our toolmaking, meaning-making natures. But Integrative Meta-perspective makes that role newly conscious and more nuanced and striking in its possibilities.

We can usefully draw on acts that are creative in the more everyday use of the word to help appreciate this at once more humble and more powerful role for awareness. A question: What becomes awareness's purpose with a great work of art or music? Is it to create the work? Given that awareness can produce only what it knows, that would not be creative at all. Is it simply to get out of the way? Such passivity has never produced anything of value. Awareness must itself function creatively.

Awareness's new definition is different from awareness's more familiar Enlightenment interpretation in the same way that the function of conscious awareness in sculpting or musical composition is different from what it might be in following a recipe. The artist's responsibility is not to craft a predefined product (no matter how elegantly)—that would not be composition. Rather, it is to help bring forth the commitment, sensitivity, and perspective needed for the artistic effort.

This new, more explicitly creative role for awareness becomes essential once reliable external guideposts stop being available—whether we are creating relationships, communities, organizations, or societies. And it becomes newly possible to manifest with Cultural Maturity's cognitive changes. We may not get to know what the ultimate outcome of our efforts will be. But we can know that anything that helps us bring these qualities to bear increases the likelihood that what results will enhance life.

Awareness's new picture redefines not just what it means to be conscious, but also what it means to be a person and the nature of leadership. The Modern Age picture made conscious awareness who we are. Awareness became that captain of the cellular ship. With leadership in the world it became truth's determiner. In the new picture, awareness remains key to what makes us human—indeed, we better appreciate what is unique in how it manifests with human experience. And it still provides leadership. But this is now leadership of a more specifically creative sort. With awareness's new definition, truth in our old triumphant, arms-length sense necessarily abandons us. We gain in exchange the ability to more deeply engage the whole of our cognitive complexity, the capacity to think more systemically, and a whole array of new creative options.

What Is a Body?

This book's observations about intelligence and its evolution have brought us close to some of life's most intriguing questions. And we've only made a start with the depth to which we could take such reflections. To get a sense of even deeper implications, let's turn to one of the most basic and primal questions we could ask: What is a body? When we think about mind and body more systemically, not only does mind in the sense of conscious awareness derive a new kind of meaning, but the word "body" also takes on a new more full and vital kind of significance. We've made a start with how I've spoken of the body as intelligent. But the implications are so fundamental that they well warrant further, more specific reflection.

On the surface, the question "What is a body?" might seem simple to answer. We need only look down; there it is. In fact, the question is not at all simple. Certainly it is perplexing philosophically. The body is at once something we have and something we are—not an easy fact to reconcile. And the question increasingly confronts us as we consider the body scientifically and medically. We are used to inquiring about how neurons work, about the biochemistry of digestion, or about the role of genes in disease. But more and more we are recognizing that we have only begun to understand the body's rich systemic complexity.

Part of the reason we have more to learn is simply that there is research yet to be done. But the reason has as much to do, ultimately, with how we think. I've observed our Modern Age tendency to view a machine model of understanding as sufficient and culminating. With our almost exclusive reliance on rational intelligence today, we can find ourselves distanced from anything but the most rudimentary action/reaction notions of bodily functioning. The extreme level of disconnection from bodily experience that we find in our time plays a role in many of today's most consequential Transitional Absurdities.

The importance of thinking of the body in more complete ways brings us back to earlier key themes. My previous emphasis on the importance of understanding living systems in ways that better reflect the fact that they are alive is certainly pertinent to how we think about the body. In particular, it is pertinent to how we conceive of bodily well-being. Health and healing must ultimately be about enhancing life. We've always known at some level that healing was more complex than fixing broken anatomy. I am reminded of Benjamin Franklin's quip, "God heals and the doctor takes the fees."

Medicine today is making a start toward elucidating a more systemic picture of bodily functioning. For example, increasingly we are recognizing how other aspects of the body than just the nervous system learn and also direct complex evolving processes. I think in particular of the immune system (which constantly creates new antibodies to fight disease), the digestive system (which manages an intricate ecosystem of supportive microorganisms), and the endocrine system (which organizes complex hormonal responses). Medicine is also better recognizing the importance of taking into account human differences—such as gender, race, and genetic variability—appreciating how the body we consider must be the body as *somebody*. While we are just beginning to grasp the full implications of this more dynamic—indeed, "creative"—picture of bodily response, we can be sure that those implications are significant. I suspect that in the twenty-first century, the body will provide many of humanity's most dramatic and important new learnings.

The basic idea that we can speak of body intelligence as I have here can be a stretch for many people. I've commented on the trickiness of doing so given that we have so little connection with the body as experience in our time. A simple thought experiment that draws on everyday experience helps make the idea that the body might be intelligent more concrete. It also provides insight with regard to another of truth's great quandaries—how to reconcile the apparent contradiction between free will and determinism.

Imagine a gifted running back in football making his way down the field, rapidly cutting this way and that. The running back's cuts take place more quickly, and in ways that are more nuanced, than could ever happen by consciously choosing them one at a time. The conscious aspects of intelligence simply aren't built to function that rapidly or complexly. Does this mean, then, that the running back is not choosing? And, more specifically, does it then mean that because his body moves before he "chooses" that what we witness is nothing more than mechanical reflex following the rules of a deterministic world? Such interpretations leave us with a less than convincing picture. At the least they leave us with bothersome questions. Are the outcomes of games then predetermined—or, alternatively, perhaps random? Either way, we are left wondering why we would attend a football game—and perhaps feeling a bit duped. I think the problem lies with the fact that our explanations really don't hold up. Clearly in the running back's movements we witness something that is not just vital, but intelligent—and profoundly so.

I've emphasized the essential role that body intelligence plays in culturally mature understanding. In particular, I've emphasized its pivotal significance in a creative picture of cognitive functioning. When we "bridge" mind and body—as culturally mature perspective always does—the question of just what it means to have a body becomes a new sort of question. It also in a whole new way becomes a question of deep significance. Creative Systems Theory not only invites us to consider a larger picture, it provides us with a way to map body realities and body dynamics.

Here, very briefly, I will draw on the theory's framing of bodily experience in a couple of ways. First, I will expand on earlier observations about the different ways that we experience bodily intelligence at various stages in culture as a creative process. I will then turn to how, with each stage in creative/formative process—including culture as a developmental process—we not only experience what it means to have a body in particular ways, but we also live in our bodies in particular ways.

It is important to appreciate that we've never really just studied the body—objectively stood back from it—even the modern scientific body. We've always studied mind/bodies, albeit of different sorts (and being mind/bodies ourselves, never from a purely objective perspective). Creative Systems Theory proposes that the way we experience our bodies at any point in time reflects a particular time-relative and space-relative relationship between mind and body. I've outlined how each intelligence—bodily intelligence included—along with being primary at a particular creative stage, makes a more limited contribution with other stages. We can add some further "flesh" to where this takes us with regard to body intelligence by making some quick observations about ways in which health and healing are experienced at each creative stage. Here is the briefest of overviews. I will limit my observations to the body as it is experienced in culture as a creative process.

I've described the Pre-Axis "creature body" culturally as the body that knows the tribal dances. It moves in harmony with the beings of the forest, the skies, and the oceans. With the Pre-Axis body, healing happens primarily through ritual and through the application of remedies found in nature. Together, they reestablish primal connectedness. The Early-Axis body tends to be described culturally in the language of energies and essences, as with the acupuncture meridians of traditional Chinese medicine and the chakras of India's yogic traditions. Healing comes then through the balancing of these energies. The Middle-Axis "visceral/muscular body" took expression in the West in interplays of emotion-laden fluids—blood, phlegm, yellow bile, black bile. (Here lie the roots of words like "bilious" and "phlegmatic.") Healing then came through removing blockages to the movements of fluids and eliminating fluids of a harmful sort. The final body in this sequence—or at least the one we know from most recent times—is our familiar Late-Axis body of anatomy and physiology, the Modern Age's body as great machine. Modern medicine views disease as damage to that machine—the cause being variously trauma, microbes, genetic defect, or wear and tear. The purpose of healing, whether through surgery or the prescribing of drugs, has been to repair broken tissues and restore their functioning.

Which of these is the real body? Were early conceptions simply naïve? In major ways, certainly they were—especially when it comes to implications for health and healing. The greater portion of the knowledge we draw on today, including discoveries as basic as the role of pathogens in disease or the importance of sterile technique, is remarkably recent. But Creative Systems Theory suggests that differences in how we've understood the body may also reflect our complexity as much as our past ignorance.

The second way of approaching who we are as bodies turns to how we can use the way bodily experience organizes creatively to help us more deeply understand creative Patterning in Time and Patterning in Space differences. In an earlier footnote, I briefly described the Creative Function. I've also noted how polar relationships manifest in ways that are more Upper and Lower, Inner and Outer. Rather than just being some abstract representation, the Creative Function depicts how polarity organizes in the human body. These differences reflect not just conceptual tendencies, but patterns of bodily organization. We can think of Creative

Systems Theory patterning concepts as describing different ways of being in our tissues. The Creative Function maps this dynamically systemic picture. It describes how what it means to be embodied evolves in a characteristic manner over the course of any formative process.

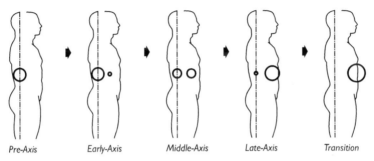

Pre-Axis   Early-Axis   Middle-Axis   Late-Axis   Transition

Fig. 6-1. The Evolution of Horizontal Polarity

The diagram in Figure 6-1—from *The Creative Imperative*—depicts how horizontal polarity manifests differently depending on when and where we find it. Creative Systems Theory describes how Inner aspects get greater emphasis early on with any formative process, while Outer sensibilities have the greater influence later on. This is consistent with what we see bodily. As we move from Pre-Axis, to Early-Axis, to Middle-Axis, to Late-Axis, embodied experience moves gradually from closer to the body's core toward the body's more surface layers. This mapping can be applied equally well to Patterning in Time and Patterning in Space observations.

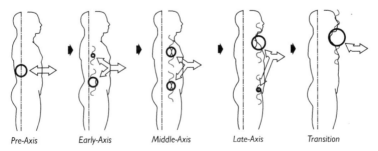

Pre-Axis   Early-Axis   Middle-Axis   Late-Axis   Transition

Fig. 6-2. The Evolution of Horizontal and Vertical Polarity

The diagram in Figure 6-2—also from *The Creative Imperative*—adds vertical polarity to the representation. Note how it makes the Creative Function specifically a mapping of embodied experience. It illustrates how horizontal and vertical polarity together generate our felt experience of ourselves and how we perceive our worlds. It similarly can be applied to both Patterning in Time and Patterning in Space observations.[3]

How does our experience of being embodied change with Integrative Meta-perspective? We become more in touch with bodily experience, certainly, better able to read our body's cues and derive fulfillment from the life of the body. There are also deeper rewards. A client described the changes this way. He observed that early in his life he had felt rooted in his beliefs. Then those beliefs were challenged, and he went through a period where he felt that he had no roots. Later, as he connected with more culturally mature sensibilities, he described in a new way feeling "rooted in the fact of rootedness." He could have said simply, rooted in his body. The way that Cultural Maturity's cognitive reordering gives us a new, more complete relationship to bodily experience is key to how Cultural Maturity provides an answer to today's Crisis of Purpose.

Advertising, Intelligence's Creative Multiplicity, and the Archetypal Function of Art

We encounter a Transitional Absurdity of particular importance at the intersection between art and advertising. It is especially pertinent to these reflections in that it provides

---

3 Creative Systems Theory uses the terms Inner and Outer rather than the more familiar words "introvert" and "extrovert" when addressing personality style differences, to avoid lumping together temperaments that are in fact fundamentally different. The diagram in Figure 6-2 points toward why more differentiated language is important. It follows from the creative organization of temperament that even the most Outer of Earlies will often be more Inner than most Lates, with the converse also being true.

a prime example of how intelligences that we have placed at arm's length can today be exploited for purposes that run wholly counter to their traditional function. Modern advertising turns the archetypal function of art on its head. That it does is of no small significance—and raises essential questions as we look to the future.

To make sense of this circumstance, we need to start by examining art's creative role in culture. Art would still be of importance if its purpose were simply to create things of beauty. But culturally mature perspective suggests that its significance is deeper—and in ways with particular pertinence to culture's emerging tasks. Art's deeper contribution follows from the fact that art takes expression from the most germinal of intelligences—the body, the imaginal, and the more internal aspects of the emotional.

That deeper contribution has a couple of parts. First, art functions as an "advocate" for, and reminder of, the more germinal aspects of intelligence tapped by the artistic endeavor and the values and sensibilities they evoke. The second kind of contribution is less obvious, but is related and has particular importance for these reflections. Art fulfills a visionary function. It connects us with new possibilities. Rainer Maria Rilke counseled the artist: "Fear not the strangeness you feel. The future must enter you before it happens." This visionary function is a product not of exceptional capacity on the part of artists (though exceptional art requires exceptional capacities), but rather of the creatively germinal intelligences that predominate in the artistic personality.

We find the most familiar example of this visionary function in how the art of the Renaissance anticipated advances in science and government that we did not see until centuries later. When we call something art, we claim that in some way it gives voice to truths just peeking over the horizon. Good or great art is art that serves this anticipatory function in especially powerful ways—in the psyche of the individual, but also, and particularly, for the "psyche of culture."

How does advertising relate to this picture of art and its contribution?

We reasonably ask what art's dominant form is today. The answer: If we define "art" in terms of the sensibilities that expression draws on, and define "dominant" in terms of dollars spent, then, hands down, today's dominant art form is advertising. (Advertising's power derives from its use of the trusted and largely invisible grammar of art—metaphor, image, movement, sound, and feeling. This power can be amplified today by how distanced the average person has become from these languages—and thus both unconscious of their workings and often hungry for their sustenance.) This answer—at once obvious and unsettling—presents an essential quandary. If art's purpose is to presage, to aesthetically lead, then advertising's ultimate effect is precisely the opposite of art, at least as defined by art's historical mandate. Advertising promotes extreme material values that can no longer serve us. And its purpose, rather than to provide insight and guidance, is to mislead, making it hardly a solution to today's Crisis of Purpose.

Put bluntly, advertising is a form of lying. Classes on advertising teach that one should never say anything logical in an advertisement—for the simple reason that doing so would encourage people to think and question (and then likely not buy the product). Instead, advertising juxtaposes images of what a person is supposed to buy with images of fulfillment: "Salems are springtime fresh" (this from when tobacco companies were well aware of smoking's health effects); "Coke is it" (as obesity becomes more and more an epidemic and diabetes ever more a scourge). Ultimately, advertising promotes our time's most dangerous lie: that consumption in and of itself brings fulfillment.

Advertising's hold on the modern psyche represents a particularly consequential kind of Transitional Absurdity. We know we are being misled, but this does not seem to diminish advertising's effect. This contradictory picture confronts us with an important follow-up leadership question: What, if we value art—and our well-being more generally—do we best do with advertising's lock on the artistic?

A person might appropriately argue that the correct answer to the follow-up "what do we do" question is that we should do nothing. If the purpose of art is to mirror what most defines culture, then advertising, given these highly materialistic times, is just art doing its job. But if art's purpose is not just to mirror, but to presage, then advertising fundamentally fails at art's task. And it ultimately fails us in a deeper way. What ultimately makes an act moral is the degree to which it supports and furthers life. Art in its dominant guise today not only fails as art, it fails the test of morality.

I am a strong advocate for media literacy curriculum in schools. The importance of having a more conscious relationship to advertising's influence is a major reason why. Advertising's capacity to inform remains an essential element in the workings of a free market and will continue to be in the future. But becoming more conscious of advertising's effects—and, when necessary, reining in its excesses—will be essential to a psychologically and spiritually healthy future. If, with Cultural Maturity's changes, we can become more conscious of and facile with the languages of aesthetic expression, we should become more capable of such creative management (both with regard to advertising and to the media more generally).[4]

---

4 Note that the machine intelligence consequence that I've argued presents today's greatest existential danger becomes much more likely—indeed, almost inevitable—when digital technologies are advertising-driven. Instructions to "maximize eyeballs" pretty much come with the business model.

AFTERWORD

Toward a New
Human Completeness

It feels a bit odd to have written a book on multiple intelligences. The fact that intelligence has multiple aspects has to me always seemed rather obvious. It was obvious to me when I was a sculptor and a musician. And it was so obvious to me as I first began to write about Creative Systems Theory that it never occurred to me that anyone would question it. But as I've suggested, not just the average person, but people for whom such awareness would seem to be essential—educators, psychologists, people in positions of social leadership—today tend to lack an appreciation for intelligence's rich multiplicity, certainly the critical importance of that multiplicity in making us who we are.

I wrote this book only after some prodding by colleagues. They reminded me that the whole idea that intelligence has multiple aspects can get rejected out of hand in certain circles. They also reminded me of the many reasons why this can't continue to be the case. In these pages, we've looked at how a fuller engagement with intelligence's creative multiplicity is needed for any at all deep sense of meaning in our time, whether personally if we are to effectively address today's Crisis of Purpose, or more broadly with the need to progress in more ultimately life-affirming ways. I've pointed toward how drawing on intelligence as a whole is required if we are to manifest the new skills and capacities necessary to successfully address any of the most important challenges ahead for the species. We've seen how a deep engagement with intelligence's creative multiplicity is needed to effectively understand history or the times we live in—and certainly it is necessary to any useful picture of the future. And I've touched on how a more complete engagement with intelligence's multiple aspects is necessary to understanding many more particular concerns with needed sophistication—such as individual differences, conscious awareness, the life of the body, human identity, or the dangers that could accompany digital technologies run amok.

We've also looked at more overarching and conceptual implications. I've described how an appreciation for intelligence's multiple aspects is needed if Integrative Metaperspective and the cultural growing up that will be so important going forward is to make real sense—or really be possible. And we've seen how the same applies to needed more dynamic and life-affirming frameworks for understanding, such as Creative Systems Theory. If intelligence's multiplicity is rejected out of hand, critical new ways of thinking are also going to be rejected out of hand.

How do we best support the needed kind of more complete engagement with intelligence's creative multiplicity? We can take time to reflect on each way of knowing and how it adds to our lives. We can also choose to engage in activities that help deepen our relationship to each of these aspects of our generative natures. We can observe how the whole of intelligence is needed to live our lives in the most complete and rewarding ways. And most important if we are to take on the task with the seriousness it deserves, we can confront how the more complete kind of understanding that becomes possible when we engage the whole of intelligence's creative multiplicity is becoming inescapably important.

I've made what might easily have seemed like an outrageous claim, that without a new, deeper relationship to intelligence's creative multiplicity we very well may be doomed. My hope is that with the book's conclusion, this claim might seem less audacious, and more simply like common sense.

INDEX

Related Recent Books By Charles Johnston

Creative Systems Theory:
A Comprehensive Theory of Purpose,
Change, and Interrelationship in Human
Systems (with Particular Pertinense to
Understanding the Times We Live In and
the Tasks Ahead for the Species)

Insight: Creative Systems Theory's
Radical New Picture of Human Possibility

Rethinking How We Think:
Integrative Meta-Perspective and the
Cognitive "Growing Up" On Which Our
Future Depends

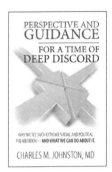

Perspective and Guidance for a Time of
Deep Discord:
Why We See Such Extreme Social and
Political Polarization—and What We Can
Do About It.

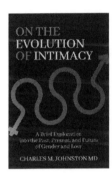

On the Evolution of Intimacy:
A Brief Exploration Into the Past,
Present, and Future of Gender and Love.

ICD Press is the publishing arm of the Institute for Creative Development. Information about the Institute and other Institute publications can be found on Charles Johnston's Author Page www.CharlesJohnstonmd.com

The Institute for Creative Development (ICD) Press
4324 Meridian Ave. N.
Seattle WA 98103
206-526-8562

Information about Dr. Johnston's ongoing work can be found on his author page (www.charlesjohnstonmd.com), on the Cultural Maturity blog (www.culturalmaturityblog.net), and on his Ask the Cultural Psychiatrist YouTube channel (youtube.com/@cjohnstonmd).

Made in the USA
Monee, IL
03 May 2023

32909075R00068